THE GOSPEL OF THE ESSENES

Oh, the Ancient Truth!
Ages upon ages past it was found,
And it bound together a Noble Brotherhood.
The Ancient Truth!
Hold fast to it!

                              − Goethe

THE GOSPEL OF THE ESSENES

THE UNKNOWN BOOKS OF THE ESSENES
&
LOST SCROLLS OF THE ESSENE BROTHERHOOD

The Original Hebrew and Aramaic Texts
translated and edited by

EDMOND BORDEAUX SZEKELY

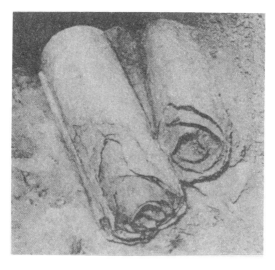

SAFFRON WALDEN
THE C. W. DANIEL CO LTD

First published in Great Britain
by The C.W. Daniel Co, Ltd.,
1 Church Path, Saffron Walden, Essex, CB1O 1JP, England
2nd impression 1979
3rd impression 1982

THE GOSPEL OF THE ESSENES
PUBLISHING HISTORY

The text of the present volume has been previously published in the
United States (1974) in two volumes with the title
The Essene Gospel of Peace
Book II: The Unknown Books of the Essenes
Book III: Lost Scrolls of the Essene Brotherhood
(Academy Books)

These editions are a sequel to Book I of the Gospel, first published in 1937
In the United Kingdom with the title
The Gospel of Peace of Jesus Christ by the Disciple John
published by The C.W. Daniel Co Ltd.
In the United States with the title
The Essene Gospel of John
(later editions: *The Essene Gospel of Peace* [I])
(Academy Books)

SBN 85207 135 3

Printed in Great Britain by
Hillman Printers (Frome) Ltd.

This Volume
containing Books Two and Three
of the Gospel of the Essenes
is dedicated to all those
who have waited patiently for forty years
in the spiritual desert of the twentieth century
for the promised land,
the continuation of Book One,
disseminated in 200,000 copies
in seventeen languages.

Book Two

THE UNKNOWN
BOOKS OF THE ESSENES

The textual content of this volume is identical with that of the original two-volume (American) edition. Introductory material, and the number and placing of illustrations have been modified to suit the present format.

CONTENTS

BOOK I

THE GOSPEL OF PEACE OF JESUS CHRIST BY THE DISCIPLE JOHN (published separately)

BOOK II

THE UNKNOWN BOOKS OF THE ESSENES

PREFACE

I have to begin this preface with a great confession: this is not my first translation of Book Two of the Essene Gospel of Peace; it is my second. The first effort took many years to complete, and it was composed painstakingly and literally, with hundreds of cross references and abundant philological and exegetical footnotes. When it was finished, I was very proud of it, and in a glow of self-satisfied accomplishment, I gave it to my friend, Aldous Huxley, to read. Two weeks later, I asked him what he thought of my monumental translation. "It is very, very bad," he answered. "It is even worse than the most boring treatises of the patristics and scholastics, which nobody reads today. It is so dry and uninteresting, in fact, that I have no desire to read Book Three." I was speechless, so he continued. "You should rewrite it, and give it some of the vitality of your other books—make it literary, readable and attractive for twentieth century readers. I'm sure the Essenes did not speak to each other in footnotes! In the form it is in now, the only readers you will have for it may be a few dogmatists in theological seminaries, who seem to take masochistic pleasure in reading this sort of thing. However," he added with a smile, "you might find some value in it as a cure for insomnia; each time I tried to read it I fell asleep in a few minutes. You might try to sell a few copies that way by advertising a new sleep remedy in the health magazines—no harmful chemicals, and all that."

It took me a long time to recuperate from his criticism. I put aside the manuscript for years. Meanwhile, I continued to receive thousands of letters from many readers from all parts of the world of my translation of Book One of the Essene Gospel of Peace, asking for the second and third books promised in the preface. Finally, I got the courage to start again. The passing of the years had mellowed my attitude and I saw my friend's criticism in a new light. I rewrote the entire manuscript, treating it as literature and poetry, coming to grips with the great problems of life, both ancient and contemporary. It was not easy to be faithful to the original, and at the same time to present the eternal truths in a way that would appeal to twentieth century man. And yet, it was vitally important that I try; for the Essenes, above all others, strove to win the hearts of men through reason, and the powerful and vivid example of their lives.

Sadly, Aldous is no longer here to read my second translation. I have a feeling he would have liked it (not a single footnote!), but I will have to leave the final judgment to my readers. If Books Two and Three will become as popular as Book One, my efforts of many, many years will be amply rewarded.

EDMOND BORDEAUX SZEKELY

San Diego, California
the first of November, 1974.

INTRODUCTION

There are three paths leading to Truth. The first is the path of the consciousness, the second that of nature, and the third is the accumulated experience of past generations, which we receive in the shape of the great masterpieces of all ages. From time immemorial, man and humanity have followed all three paths.

The first path to Truth, the path of the consciousness, is that followed by the great mystics. They consider that the consciousness is the most immediate reality for us and is the key to the universe. It is something which is in us, which *is* us. And throughout the ages the mystics have made the discovery that the laws of human consciousness contain an aspect not found in the laws governing the material universe.

A certain dynamic unity exists in our consciousness, where one is at the same time many. It is possible for us to have simultaneously different thoughts, ideas, associations, images, memories and intuitions occupying our consciousness within fragments of a minute or a second, yet all this multiplicity will still constitute only a single dynamic unity. Therefore the laws of mathematics, which are valid for the material universe and are a key to its understanding, will not be valid in the field of consciousness, a realm where two and two do not necessarily make four. The mystics also found that measurements of space, time and weight, universally valid in nature and throughout the material universe, are not applicable to the consciousness, where sometimes a few seconds seem like hours, or hours like a minute.

Our consciousness does not exist in space and therefore cannot be measured in spatial terms. It has its own time, which is very often timelessness, so temporal measurements cannot be applied to Truth reached by this path. The great mystics discovered that the human consciousness, besides being the most immediate and the inmost reality for us, is at the same time our closest source of energy, harmony and knowledge. The path to Truth leading to and through the consciousness produced the great teachings of humanity, the great intuitions and the great masterpieces throughout the ages. Such then is the first path to or source of Truth, as the Essene traditions understand and interpret it.

Unfortunately, the magnificent original intuitions of the great masters often lose their vitality as they pass down the generations. They are very often modified, distorted and turned into dogmas, and all too frequently their values become petrified in institutions and organized hierarchies. The pure intuitions are choked by the sands of time, and eventually have to be dug out by seekers of Truth able to penetrate into their essence.

Another danger is that persons following this path to Truth—the path of the consciousness—may fall into exaggerations. They come to think that this is the only path to Truth and disregard all others. Very often, too, they apply the specific laws of the human consciousness to the material universe where they lack validity, and ignore the laws proper to the latter sphere. The mystic often creates for himself an artificial universe, farther and farther removed from reality, till he ends by living in an ivory tower, having lost all contact with reality and life.

The second of the three paths is the path of nature. While the first path of the consciousness starts from within and penetrates thence into the totality of things, the second path takes the opposite way. Its starting point is the external world. It is the path of the scientist, and has been followed in all ages through experience and through experiment, through the use of inductive and deductive methods. The scientist, working with exact quantitative measurements, measures everything in space and time, and makes all possible correlations.

With his telescope he penetrates into far-distant cosmic space, into the various solar and galactic systems; through spectrum analysis he measures the constituents of the different planets in cosmic space; and by mathematical calculation he establishes in advance the movements of celestial bodies. Applying the law of cause and effect, the scientist establishes a long chain of causes and effects which help him to explain and measure the universe, as well as life.

But the scientist, like the mystic, sometimes falls into exaggerations. While science has transformed the life of mankind and has created great values for man in all ages, it has failed to give entire satisfaction in the solution of the final problems of existence, life and the universe. The scientist has the long chain of causes and effects secure in all its particles, but he has no idea what to do with the end of the chain. He has no solid point to which he may attach the end of the chain, and so by the path to Truth through nature and the material universe he is unable to answer the great and eternal questions concerning the beginning and end of all things.

The greatest scientists recognize that in the metaphysical field beyond the scientific chain there is something else—continuing from the end of that chain. However, there are also the dogmatic scientists who deny any other approach to Truth than their own, who refuse to attribute reality to the facts and phenomena which they cannot fit neatly into their own categories and classifications.

The path to Truth through nature is not that of the dogmatic scientist, just as the first path is not that of the one-sided mystic. Nature is a great open book in which everything can be found, if we learn to draw from it the inspiration which it has given to the great thinkers of all ages. If we learn her language, nature will reveal to us all the laws of life and the universe.

It is for this reason that all the great masters of humanity from time to time withdrew into nature: Zarathustra and Moses into the mountains, Buddha to the forest, Jesus and the Essenes to the desert—and thus followed this second path as well as that of the consciousness. The two paths do not contradict one another, but harmoniously complete one another in full knowledge of the laws of both. It was thus that the great teachers reached wonderful and deeply profound truths which have given inspiration to millions through thousands of years.

The third path to Truth, is the wisdom, knowledge and experience acquired by the great thinkers of all ages and transmitted to us in the form of great teachings, the great sacred books or scriptures, and the great masterpieces of universal literature which together form what today we would call universal culture. In brief, therefore, our approach to Truth is a threefold one: through consciousness, nature and culture.

In the following chapters we shall follow this threefold path leading to Truth and shall examine and translate some of the great sacred writings of the Essenes.

There are different ways of studying these great writings. One way—the way of all theologians and of the organized Churches—is to consider each text literally. This is the dogmatic way resulting from a long process of petrification, by which truths are inevitably transformed into dogmas.

When the theologian follows this most easy but one-sided path, he runs into endless contradictions and complications, and he reaches a conclusion as far removed from the truth as that of the scientific interpreter of these texts who rejects them as entirely valueless and without validity. The approaches of the dogmatic theologian and the exclusivist scientist represent two extremes.

A third error is to believe, as do certain symbolists, that these books have no more than a symbolic content and are nothing more than parables. With their own particular way of exaggeration these symbolists make thousands of different and quite contradictory interpretations of these great texts. The spirit of the Essene traditions is opposed to all three of these ways of interpreting these ageless writings and follows an entirely different approach.

The Essene method of interpretation of these books is, on the one hand, to place them in harmonious correlation with the laws of the human consciousness and of nature, and, on the other, to consider the facts and circumstances of the age and environment in which they were written. This approach also takes into account the degree of evolution and understanding of the people to whom the particular master was addressing his message.

Since all the great masters had to adapt their teaching to the level of their audience, they found it necessary to formulate both an exoteric and esoteric teaching. The exoteric message was one comprehensible to the people at large and was expressed in terms of various rules, forms and rituals corresponding to the basic needs of the people and the age concerned. Parallel with this, the esoteric teachings have survived through the ages partly as written and partly as unwritten living traditions, free from forms, rituals, rules and dogmas, and in all periods have been kept alive and practised by a small minority.

It is in this spirit of the interpretation of the Truth that the Essene Gospel of Peace will be translated in the following pages. Rejecting the dogmatic methods of literal and purely scientific interpretation as well as the exaggeration of the symbolists, we shall try to translate the Essene Gospel of Peace in the light of our consciousness and of nature, and in harmony with the great traditions of the Essenes, to whose brotherhood the authors of the Dead Sea Scrolls themselves belonged.

THE VISION OF ENOCH

THE MOST ANCIENT REVELATION

God Speaks to Man

I speak to you.
Be still
Know
I am
God.

I spoke to you
When you were born.
Be still
Know
I am
God.

I spoke to you
At your first sight.
Be still
Know
I am
God.

I spoke to you
At your first word.
Be still
Know
I am
God.

I spoke to you
At your first thought.
Be still
Know
I am
God.

I spoke to you
At your first love.
Be still
Know
I am
God.

I spoke to you
At your first song.
Be still
Know
I am
God.

I speak to you
Through the grass of the meadows.
Be still
Know
I am
God.

I speak to you
Through the trees of the forests.
Be still
Know

I am
God.

I speak to you
Through the valleys and the hills.
Be still
Know
I am
God.

I speak to you
Through the Holy Mountains.
Be still
Know
I am
God.

I speak to you
Through the rain and the snow.
Be still
Know
I am
God.

I speak to you
Through the waves of the sea.
Be still
Know
I am
God.

I speak to you

Through the dew of the morning.
Be still
Know
I am
God.

I speak to you
Through the peace of the evening.
Be still
Know
I am
God.

I speak to you
Through the splendor of the sun.
Be still
Know
I am
God.

I speak to you
Through the brilliant stars.
Be still
Know
I am
God.

I speak to you
Through the storm and the clouds.
Be still
Know
I am

God.

I speak to you
Through the thunder and lightning.
Be still
Know
I am
God.

I speak to you
Through the mysterious rainbow.
Be still
Know
I am
God.

I will speak to you
When you are alone.
Be still
Know
I am
God.

I will speak to you
Through the Wisdom of the Ancients.
Be still
Know
I am
God.

I will speak to you
At the end of time.

Be still
Know
I am
God.

I will speak to you
When you have seen my Angels.
Be still
Know
I am
God.

I will speak to you
Throughout Eternity.
Be still
Know
I am
God.

I speak to you.
Be still
Know
I am
God.

THE TEN COMMANDMENTS

And Mount Sinai was altogether in smoke because the Lord descended upon it in fire: and the smoke thereof ascended as the smoke of a furnace, and the whole mount quaked greatly.

And the Lord came down upon Mount Sinai, on the top of the mount: and the Lord called Moses up to the top of the mount: and Moses went up.

And the Lord called unto Moses out of the mountain, saying, Come unto me, for I would give thee the Law for thy people, which shall be a covenant for the Children of Light.

And Moses went up unto God. And God spake all these words, saying,

I am the Law, thy God, which hath brought thee out from the depths of the bondage of darkness.

Thou shalt have no other Laws before me.

Thou shalt not make unto thee any image of the Law in heaven above or in the earth beneath. I am the invisible Law, without beginning and without end.

Thou shalt not make unto thee false laws, for I am the Law, and the whole Law of all laws. If thou forsake me, thou shalt be visited by disasters for generation upon generation.

If thou keepest my commandments, thou shalt enter the Infinite Garden where stands the Tree of Life in the midst of the Eternal Sea.

Thou shalt not violate the Law. The Law is thy God, who shall not hold thee guiltless.

Honor thy Earthly Mother, that thy days may be long upon the land, and honor thy Heavenly Father, that eternal life be thine in the heavens, for the earth and the heavens are given unto thee by the Law, which is thy God.

Thou shalt greet thy Earthly Mother on the morning of the Sabbath.

Thou shalt greet the Angel of Earth on the second morning.

Thou shalt greet the Angel of Life on the third morning.

Thou shalt greet the Angel of Joy on the fourth morning.
Thou shalt greet the Angel of Sun on the fifth morning.
Thou shalt greet the Angel of Water on the sixth morning.
Thou shalt greet the Angel of Air on the seventh morning.

All these Angels of the Earthly Mother shalt thou greet, and consecrate thyself to them, that thou mayest enter the Infinite Garden where stands the Tree of Life.

Thou shalt worship thy Heavenly Father on the evening
of the Sabbath.

Thou shalt commune with the Angel of Eternal Life on
the second evening.

Thou shalt commune with the Angel of Work on the third
evening.

Thou shalt commune with the Angel of Peace on the fourth
evening.

Thou shalt commune with the Angel of Power on the
fifth evening.

Thou shalt commune with the Angel of Love on the sixth
evening.

Thou shalt commune with the Angel of Wisdom on the
seventh evening.

All these Angels of the Heavenly Father shalt thou commune with, that thy soul may bathe in the Fountain of Light, and enter into the Sea of Eternity.

The seventh day is the Sabbath: thou shalt remember it, and keep it holy. The Sabbath is the day of the Light of the Law, thy God. In it thou shalt not do any work, but search the Light, the Kingdom of thy God, and all things shall be given unto thee.

For know ye that during six days thou shalt work with the Angels, but the seventh day shalt thou dwell in the Light of thy Lord, who is the holy Law.

Thou shalt not take the life from any living thing. Life comes only from God, who giveth it and taketh it away.

Thou shalt not debase Love. It is the sacred gift of thy Heavenly Father.

Thou shalt not trade thy Soul, the priceless gift of the loving

God, for the riches of the world, which are as seeds sown on stony ground, having no root in themselves, and so enduring but for a little while.

Thou shalt not be a false witness of the Law, to use it against thy brother: Only God knoweth the beginning and the ending of all things, for his eye is single, and he is the holy Law.

Thou shalt not covet thy neighbor's possessions. The Law giveth unto thee much greater gifts, even the earth and the heavens, if thou keep the Commandments of the Lord thy God.

And Moses heard the voice of the Lord, and sealed within him the covenant that was between the Lord and the Children of Light.

And Moses turned, and went down from the mount, and the two tablets of the Law were in his hand.

And the tablets were the work of God, and the writing was the writing of God, graven upon the tablets.

And the people knew not what became of Moses, and they gathered themselves together and brake off their golden earrings and made a molten calf. And they worshipped unto the idol, and offered to it burnt offerings.

And they ate and drank and danced before the golden calf, which they had made, and they abandoned themselves to corruption and evil before the Lord.

And it came to pass, as soon as he came nigh unto the camp, that he saw the calf, and the dancing, and the wickedness of the people: and Moses' anger waxed hot, and he cast the tablets out of his hands, and brake them beneath the mount.

And it came to pass on the morrow, that Moses said unto the people, Ye have sinned a great sin, ye have denied thy Creator. I will go up unto the Lord and plead atonement for thy sin.

And Moses returned unto the Lord, and said, Lord, thou hast seen the desecration of thy Holy Law. For thy children lost faith, and worshipped the darkness, and made for themselves a golden calf. Lord, forgive them, for they are blind to the light.

And the Lord said unto Moses, *Behold, at the beginning of time was a covenant made between God and man, and the holy flame of the Creator did enter unto him. And he was made the son of*

God, and it was given him to guard his inheritance of the first-born, and to make fruitful the land of his Father and keep it holy. And he who casteth out the Creator from him doth spit upon his birthright, and no more grievous sin doth exist in the eyes of God.

And the Lord spoke, saying, *Only the Children of Light can keep the Commandments of the Law. Hear me, for I say thus: the tablets which thou didst break, these shall nevermore be written in the words of men. As thou didst return them to the earth and fire, so shall they live, invisible, in the hearts of those who are able to follow their Law. To thy people of little faith, who did sin against the Creator, even whilst thou stood on holy ground before thy God, I will give another Law. It shall be a stern law, yea, it shall bind them, for they know not yet the Kingdom of Light.*

And Moses hid the invisible Law within his breast, and kept it for a sign to the Children of Light. And God gave unto Moses the written law for the people, and he went down unto them, and spake unto them with a heavy heart.

And Moses said unto the people, these are the laws which thy God hath given thee.

Thou shalt have no other gods before me.

Thou shalt not make unto thee any graven image.

Thou shalt not take the name of the Lord thy God in vain.

Remember the Sabbath day, to keep it holy.

Honor thy father and thy mother.

Thou shalt not kill.

Thou shalt not commit adultery.

Thou shalt not steal.

Thou shalt not bear false witness against thy neighbor.

Thou shalt not covet thy neighbor's house, nor thy neighbor's wife, nor anything that is thy neighbor's.

And there was a day of mourning and atonement for the great sin against the Creator, which did not end. And the broken tablets of the Invisible Law lived hidden in the breast of Moses, until it came to pass that the Children of Light appeared in the desert, and the angels walked the earth.

And it was by the bed of a stream, that the weary and afflicted came again to seek out Jesus. And like children, they had forgotten the Law; and like children, they sought out their father to show them where they had erred, and to set their feet again upon the path. And when the sun rose over the earth's rim they saw Jesus coming toward them from the mountain, with the brightness of the rising sun about his head.

And he raised his hand and smiled upon them, saying, "Peace be with you."

But they were ashamed to return his greeting, for each in his own way had turned his back on the holy teachings, and the Angels of the Earthly Mother and the Heavenly Father were not with them. And one man looked up in anguish and spoke: "Master, we are in sore need of your wisdom. For we know that which is good, and yet we follow evil. We know that to enter the kingdom of heaven we must walk with the angels of the day and of the night, yet our feet walk in the ways of the wicked. The light of day shines only on our pursuit of pleasure, and the night falls on our heedless stupor. Tell us, Master, how may we talk with the angels, and stay within their holy circle, that the Law may burn in our hearts with a constant flame?"

And Jesus spoke to them:

> *"To lift your eyes to heaven*
> *When all mens' eyes are on the ground,*
> *Is not easy.*
> *To worship at the feet of the angels*
> *When all men worship only fame and riches,*
> *Is not easy.*
> *But the most difficult of all*
> *Is to think the thoughts of the angels,*
> *To speak the words of the angels,*
> *And to do as angels do."*

And one man spoke: "But, Master, we are but men, we are not angels. How then can we hope to walk in their ways? Tell us what we must do."

And Jesus spoke:

> *"As the son inherits the land of his father,*
> *So have we inherited a Holy Land*
> *From our Fathers.*
> *This land is not a field to be ploughed,*
> *But a place within us*
> *Where we may build our Holy Temple.*
> *And even as a temple must be raised,*
> *Stone by stone,*
> *So will I give to you those stones*
> *For the building of the Holy Temple;*
> *That which we have inherited*
> *From our Fathers,*
> *And their Fathers' Fathers."*

And all the men gathered around Jesus, and their faces shone with desire to hear the words which would come from his lips. And he lifted his face to the rising sun, and the radiance of its rays filled his eyes as he spoke:

> *"The Holy Temple can be built*
> *Only with the ancient Communions,*
> *Those which are spoken,*
> *Those which are thought,*
> *And those which are lived.*
> *For if they are spoken only with the mouth,*
> *They are as a dead hive*
> *Which the bees have forsaken,*
> *That gives no more honey.*
> *The Communions are a bridge*
> *Between man and the angels,*

And like a bridge,
Can be built only with patience,
Yea, even as the bridge over the river
Is fashioned stone by stone,
As they are found by the water's edge.

And the Communions are fourteen in number,
As the Angels of the Heavenly Father
Number seven,
And the Angels of the Earthly Mother
Number seven.
And just as the roots of the tree
Sink into the earth and are nourished,
And the branches of the tree
Raise their arms to heaven,
So is man like the trunk of the tree,
With his roots deep
In the breast of his Earthly Mother,
And his soul ascending
To the bright stars of his Heavenly Father.
And the roots of the tree
Are the Angels of the Earthly Mother,
And the branches of the tree
Are the Angels of the Heavenly Father.
And this is the sacred Tree of Life
Which stands in the Sea of Eternity.

The first Communion is with
The Angel of Sun,
She who cometh each morning
As a bride from her chamber,
To shed her golden light on the world.
O thou immortal, shining, swift-steeded

Angel of the Sun!
There is no warmth without thee,
No fire without thee,
No life without thee.
The green leaves of the trees
Do worship thee,
And through thee is the tiny wheat kernel
Become a river of golden grass,
Moving with the wind.
Through thee is opened the flower
In the center of my body.
Therefore will I never hide myself
From thee.
Angel of Sun,
Holy messenger of the Earthly Mother,
Enter the holy temple within me
And give me the Fire of Life!

The second Communion is with
The Angel of Water,
She who makes the rain
To fall on the arid plain,
Who fills the dry well to overflowing.
Yea, we do worship thee,
Water of Life.
From the heavenly sea
The waters run and flow forward
From the never-failing springs.
In my blood flow
A thousand pure springs,
And vapors, and clouds,
And all the waters

That spread over all the seven Kingdoms.
All the waters
The Creator hath made
Are holy.
The voice of the Lord
Is upon the waters:
The God of Glory thundereth;
The Lord is upon many waters.
Angel of Water,
Holy messenger of the Earthly Mother,
Enter the blood that flows through me,
Wash my body in the rain
That falls from heaven,
And give me the Water of Life!

The third Communion is with
The Angel of Air,
Who spreads the perfume
Of sweet-smelling fields,
Of spring grass after rain,
Of the opening buds of the
Rose of Sharon.
We worship the Holy Breath
Which is placed higher
Than all the other things created.
For, lo, the eternal and sovereign
Luminous space,
Where rule the unnumbered stars,
Is the air we breathe in
And the air we breathe out.
And in the moment betwixt the breathing in
And the breathing out

Is hidden all the mysteries
Of the Infinite Garden.
Angel of Air,
Holy messenger of the Earthly Mother,
Enter deep within me,
As the swallow plummets from the sky,
That I may know the secrets of the wind
And the music of the stars.

The fourth Communion is with
The Angel of Earth,
She who brings forth corn and grapes
From the fulness of the earth,
She who brings children
From the loins of husband and wife.
He who would till the earth,
With the left arm and the right,
Unto him will she bring forth
An abundance of fruit and grain,
Golden-hued plants
Growing up from the earth
During the spring,
As far as the earth extends,
As far as the rivers stretch,
As far as the sun rises,
To impart their gifts of food unto men.
This wide earth do I praise,
Expanded far with paths,
The productive, the full-bearing,
Thy Mother, holy plant!
Yea, I praise the lands
Where thou dost grow,

Sweet-scented, swiftly spreading,
The good growth of the Lord.
He who sows corn, grass and fruit,
Soweth the Law.
And his harvest shall be bountiful,
And his crop shall be ripe upon the hills.
As a reward for the followers of the Law,
The Lord sent the Angel of Earth,
Holy messenger of the Earthly Mother,
To make the plants to grow,
And to make fertile the womb of woman,
That the earth may never be without
The laughter of children.
Let us worship the Lord in her!

The fifth Communion is with
The Angel of Life,
She who gives strength and vigor to man.
For, lo, if the wax is not pure,
How then can the candle give a steady flame?
Go, then, toward the high-growing trees,
And before one of them which is beautiful,
High-growing and mighty,
Say these words:
'Hail be unto thee! O good, living tree,
Made by the Creator!'
Then shall the River of Life
Flow between you and your Brother,
The Tree,
And health of the body,
Swiftness of foot,
Quick hearing of the ears,

Strength of the arms
And eyesight of the eagle be yours.
Such is the Communion
With the Angel of Life,
Holy messenger of the Earthly Mother.

The sixth Communion is with
The Angel of Joy,
She who descends upon earth
To give beauty to all men.
For the Lord is not worshipped with sadness,
Nor with cries of despair.
Leave off your moans and lamentations,
And sing unto the Lord a new song:
Sing unto the Lord, all the earth.
Let the heavens rejoice
And let the earth be glad.
Let the field be joyful,
Let the floods clap their hands,
Let the hills be joyful together
Before the Lord.
For you shall go out with joy
And be led forth with peace:
The mountains and the hills
Shall break forth before you into singing.
Angel of Joy,
Holy messenger of the Earthly Mother,
I will sing unto the Lord
As long as I live:
I will sing praise to my God
While I have my being.

The seventh Communion is with
Our Earthly Mother,
She who sends forth her Angels
To guide the roots of man
And send them deep into the blessed soil.
We invoke the Earthly Mother!
The Holy Preserver!
The Maintainer!
It is She who will restore the world!
The earth is hers,
And the fulness thereof the world,
And they that dwell therein.
We worship the good, the strong,
The beneficent Earthly Mother
And all her Angels,
Bounteous, valiant,
And full of strength;
Welfare-bestowing, kind,
And health-giving.
Through her brightness and glory
Do the plants grow up from the earth,
By the never-failing springs.
Through her brightness and glory
Do the winds blow,
Driving down the clouds
Towards the never-failing springs.
The Earthly Mother and I are One.
I have my roots in her,
And she takes her delight in me,
According to the Holy Law."

Then there was a great silence, as the listeners pondered the words of Jesus. And there was new strength in them, and desire and hope shone in their faces. And then one man spoke: "Master, we are filled with eagerness to begin our Communions with the Angels of the Earthly Mother, who planted the Great Garden of the Earth. But what of the Angels of the Heavenly Father, who rule the night? How are we to talk to them, who are so far above us, who are invisible to our eyes? For we can see the rays of the sun, we can feel the cool water of the stream where we bathe, and the grapes are warm to our touch as they grow purple on the vines. But the Angels of the Heavenly Father cannot be seen, or heard, or touched. How then can we talk to them, and enter their Infinite Garden? Master, tell us what we must do."

And the morning sun encircled his head with glory as Jesus looked upon them and spoke:

> *"My children, know you not that the Earth*
> *And all that dwells therein*
> *Is but a reflection of the*
> *Kingdom of the Heavenly Father?*
> *And as you are suckled and comforted*
> *By your mother when a child,*
> *But go to join your father in the fields*
> *When you grow up,*
> *So do the Angels of the Earthly Mother*
> *Guide your steps*
> *Toward him who is your Father,*
> *And all his holy Angels,*
> *That you may know your true home*
> *And become true Sons of God.*
> *While we are children,*
> *We will see the rays of the sun,*
> *But not the Power which created it;*
> *While we are children,*
> *We will hear the sounds of the flowing brook,*
> *But not the Love which created it;*

While we are children,
We will see the stars,
But not the hand which scatters them
Through the sky,
As the farmer scatters his seed.
Only through the Communions
With the Angels of the Heavenly Father,
Will we learn to see the unseen,
To hear that which cannot be heard,
And to speak the unspoken word.

The first Communion is with
The Angel of Power,
Who fills the sun with heat,
And guides the hand of man
In all his works.
Thine, O Heavenly Father!
Was the Power,
When thou didst order a path
For each of us and all.
Through thy power
Will my feet tread the
Path of the Law;
Through thy power
Will my hands perform thy works.
May the golden river of power
Always flow from thee to me,
And may my body always turn unto thee,
As the flower turns unto the sun.
For there is no power save that
From the Heavenly Father;
All else is but a dream of dust,

A cloud passing over the face of the sun.
There is no man that hath power
Over the spirit;
Neither hath he power in the day of death.
Only that power which cometh from God
Can carry us out from the City of Death.
Guide our works and deeds,
O Angel of Power,
Holy messenger of the Heavenly Father!

The second Communion is with
The Angel of Love,
Whose healing waters flow
In a never-ending stream
From the Sea of Eternity.
Beloved, let us love one another:
For love is of the Heavenly Father,
And every one that loveth
Is born of the Heavenly Order
And knoweth the Angels.
For without love,
A man's heart is parched and cracked
As the bottom of a dry well,
And his words are empty
As a hollow gourd.
But loving words are as a honeycomb
Sweet to the soul;
Loving words in a man's mouth
Are as deep waters,
And the wellspring of love
As a flowing brook.
Yea, it was said in the ancient of days,

Thou shalt love thy Heavenly Father
With all thy heart,
And with all thy mind,
And with all thy deeds,
And thou shalt love thy brothers
As thyself.
The Heavenly Father is love;
And he that dwelleth in love
Dwelleth in the Heavenly Father,
And the Heavenly Father in him.
He that loveth not is as a wandering bird
Cast out of the nest;
For him the grass faileth
And the stream has a bitter taste.
And if a man say,
I love the Heavenly Father
But hate my brother,
He is a liar:
For he that loveth not his brother
Whom he hath seen,
How can he love the Heavenly Father
Whom he hath not seen?
By this we know the Children of Light:
Those who walk with the Angel of Love,
For they love the Heavenly Father,
And they love their brethren,
And they keep the Holy Law.
Love is stronger
Than the currents of deep waters:
Love is stronger than death.

The third Communion is with

The Angel of Wisdom,
Who maketh man free from fear,
Wide of heart,
And easy of conscience:
Holy Wisdom,
The Understanding that unfolds,
Continuously,
As a holy scroll,
Yet does not come through learning.
All wisdom cometh
From the Heavenly Father,
And is with him for ever.
Who can number the sand of the sea,
And the drops of rain,
And the days of eternity?
Who can find out the height of heaven,
And the breadth of the earth?
Who can tell the beginning
Of wisdom?
Wisdom hath been created
Before all things.
He who is without wisdom
Is like unto him that saith to the wood,
'Awake', and to the dumb stone,
'Arise, and teach!'
So are his words empty,
And his deeds harmful,
As a child who brandishes his father's sword
And knoweth not its cutting edge.
But the crown of wisdom
Makes peace and perfect health
To flourish,

Both of which are the gifts of God.
O thou Heavenly Order!
And thou, Angel of Wisdom!
I will worship thee and
The Heavenly Father,
Because of whom
The river of thought within us
Is flowing towards the
Holy Sea of Eternity.

The fourth Communion is with
The Angel of Eternal Life,
Who brings the message of eternity
To man.
For he who walks with the Angels
Shall learn to soar
Above the clouds,
And his home shall be
In the Eternal Sea
Where stands the sacred Tree of Life.
Do not wait for death
To reveal the great mystery;
If you know not your Heavenly Father
While your feet tread the dusty soil,
There shall be naught but shadows for thee
In the life that is to come.
Here and now
Is the mystery revealed.
Here and now
Is the curtain lifted.
Be not afraid, O man!
Lay hold of the wings of the

Angel of Eternal Life,
And soar into the paths of the stars,
The moon, the sun,
And the endless Light,
Moving around in their
Revolving circle forever,
And fly toward the Heavenly Sea
Of Eternal Life.

The fifth Communion is with
The Angel of Work,
Who sings in the humming of the bee,
Pausing not in its making of golden honey;
In the flute of the shepherd,
Who sleeps not lest his flock go astray;
In the song of the maiden
As she lays her hand to the spindle.
And if you think that these
Are not as fair in the eyes of the Lord
As the loftiest of prayers
Echoed from the highest mountain,
Then you do indeed err.
For the honest work of humble hands
Is a daily prayer of thanksgiving,
And the music of the plough
Is a joyful song unto the Lord.
He who eats the bread of idleness
Must die of hunger,
For a field of stones
Can yield only stones.
For him is the day without meaning,
And the night a bitter journey of evil dreams.

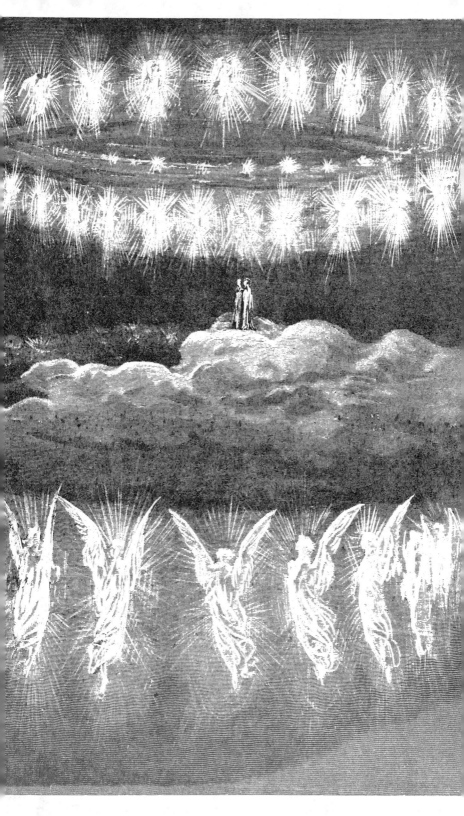

The mind of the idle
Is full of the weeds of discontent;
But he who walks with the
Angel of Work
Has within him a field always fertile,
Where corn and grapes
And all manner of sweet-scented
Herbs and flowers grow in abundance.
As ye sow, so shall ye reap.
The man of God who has found his task
Shall not ask any other blessing.

The sixth Communion is with
The Angel of Peace,
Whose kiss bestoweth calm,
And whose face is as the surface
Of untroubled waters,
Wherein the moon is reflected.
I will invoke Peace,
Whose breath is friendly,
Whose hand smooths the troubled brow.
In the reign of Peace,
There is neither hunger nor thirst,
Neither cold wind nor hot wind,
Neither old age nor death.
But to him that hath not peace in his soul,
There is no place to build within
The Holy Temple;
For how can the carpenter build
In the midst of a whirlwind?
The seed of violence can reap
Only a harvest of desolation,

And from the parched clay
Can grow no living thing.
Seek ye then the Angel of Peace,
Who is as the morning star
In the midst of a cloud,
As the moon at the full,
As a fair olive tree budding forth fruit,
And as the sun shining on the temple
Of the most High.
Peace dwells in the heart of silence:
Be still, and know that I am God.

The seventh Communion is with
The Heavenly Father,
Who is,
Who was, and
Who ever shall be.
O Great Creator!
Thou didst create the Heavenly Angels,
And thou didst reveal the
Heavenly Laws!
Thou art my refuge and my fortress,
Thou art from everlasting.
Lord, thou hast been our dwelling place
In all generations.
Before the mountains were brought forth,
Or ever thou hadst formed the earth,
Even from everlasting to everlasting,
Thou art God.
Who hath made the waters,
And who maketh the plants?
Who to the wind

Hath yoked the storm-clouds,
The swift and even the fleetest?
Who, O Great Creator!
Is the fountain of Eternal Life
Within our souls?
Who hath made the Light and the Darkness?
Who hath made sleep
And the zest of the waking hours?
Who spread the noontides
And the midnight?
Thou, O Great Creator!
Thou hast made the earth
By thy power,
Hath established the world
By thy wisdom,
And hath stretched out the heavens
By thy love.
Do thou reveal unto me,
O Heavenly Father,
Thy nature,
Which is the power of the
Angels of thy Holy Kingdom.
Immortality and the Heavenly Order
Hast thou given, O Creator,
And the best of all things,
Thy Holy Law!
I will praise thy works
With songs of thanksgiving,
Continually,
In all the generations of time.
With the coming of day
I embrace my Mother,

With the coming of night,
I join my Father,
And with the outgoing
Of evening and morning
I will breathe Their Law,
And I will not interrupt these Communions
Until the end of time."

And over heaven and earth was a great silence, and the peace of the Heavenly Father and the Earthly Mother shone over the heads of Jesus and the multitude.

THE SEVENFOLD PEACE

And seeing the multitudes, Jesus went up into a mountain, and his disciples came unto him, and all those who hungered for his words. And seeing them gathered, he opened his mouth and taught them, saying:

"Peace I bring to thee, my children,
The Sevenfold Peace
Of the Earthly Mother
And the Heavenly Father.
Peace I bring to thy body,
Guided by the Angel of Power;
Peace I bring to thy heart,
Guided by the Angel of Love;
Peace I bring to thy mind,
Guided by the Angel of Wisdom.
Through the Angels of
Power, Love and Wisdom,
Thou shalt travel the Seven Paths
Of the Infinite Garden,
And thy body, thy heart and thy mind
Shall join in Oneness
In the Sacred Flight to the
Heavenly Sea of Peace.

Yea, I tell thee truly,
The paths are seven
Through the Infinite Garden,
And each must be traversed
By the body, the heart and the mind
As one,
Lest thou stumble and fall

Into the abyss of emptiness.
For as a bird cannot fly with one wing,
So doth thy Bird of Wisdom
Need two wings of Power and Love
To soar above the abyss
To the Holy Tree of Life.

For the body alone
Is an abandoned house seen from afar:
What was thought beautiful
Is but ruin and desolation
When drawing near.
The body alone
Is as a chariot fashioned from gold,
Whose maker sets it on a pedestal,
Loath to soil it with use.
But as a golden idol,
It is ugly and without grace,
For only in movement
Doth it reveal its purpose.
Like the hollow blackness of a window
When the wind puts out its candle,
Is the body alone,
With no heart and no mind
To fill it with light.

And the heart alone
Is a sun with no earth to shine upon,
A light in the void,
A ball of warmth drowned
In a sea of blackness.
For when a man doth love,
That love turneth only to

Its own destruction
When there is no hand to stretch forth
In good works,
And no mind to weave the flames of desire
Into a tapestry of psalms.
Like a whirlwind in the desert
Is the heart alone,
With no body and no mind
To lead it singing
Through the cypress and the pine.

And the mind alone
Is a holy scroll
Which has worn thin with the years,
And must be buried.
The truth and beauty of its words
Have not changed,
But the eyes can no longer read
The faded letters,
And it falleth to pieces in the hands.
So is the mind without the heart
To give it words,
And without the body
To do its deeds.
For what availeth wisdom
Without a heart to feel
And a tongue to give it voice?
Barren as the womb of an aged woman
Is the mind alone,
With no heart and no body
To fill it with life.

For, lo, I tell thee truly,

The body and the heart and the mind
Are as a chariot, and a horse, and a driver.
The chariot is the body,
Forged in strength to do the will
Of the Heavenly Father
And the Earthly Mother.
The heart is the fiery steed,
Glorious and courageous,
Who carries the chariot bravely,
Whether the road be smooth,
Or whether stones and fallen trees
Lie in its path.
And the driver is the mind,
Holding the reins of wisdom,
Seeing from above what lieth
On the far horizon,
Charting the course of hoofs and wheels.

Give ear, O ye heavens,
And I will speak;
And hear, O earth,
The words of my mouth.
My doctrine shall drop as the rain,
My speech shall distil as the dew,
As the small rain
Upon the tender herb,
And as the showers upon the grass.

Blessed is the Child of Light
Who is strong in body,
For he shall have oneness with the earth.
Thou shalt celebrate a daily feast
With all the gifts of the Angel of Earth:

The golden wheat and corn,
The purple grapes of autumn,
The ripe fruits of the trees,
The amber honey of the bees.
Thou shalt seek the fresh air
Of the forest and of the fields,
And there in the midst of them
Shalt thou find the Angel of Air.
Put off thy shoes and clothing
And suffer the Angel of Air
To embrace all thy body.
Then shalt thou breathe long and deeply,
That the Angel of Air
May be brought within thee.
Enter into the cool and flowing river
And suffer the Angel of Water
To embrace all thy body.
Cast thyself wholly into his enfolding arms,
And as often as thou movest the air
With thy breath,
Move with thy body the water also.
Thou shalt seek the Angel of Sun,
And enter into that embrace
Which doth purify with holy flames.
And all these things are of the Holy Law
Of the Earthly Mother,
She who did give thee birth.
He who hath found peace with the body
Hath built a holy temple
Wherein may dwell forever
The spirit of God.
Know this peace with thy mind,

Desire this peace with thy heart,
Fulfill this peace with thy body.

Blessed is the Child of Light
Who is wise in mind,
For he shall create heaven.
The mind of the wise
Is a well-ploughed field,
Which giveth forth abundance and plenty.
For it thou showest a handful of seed
To a wise man,
He will see in his mind's eye
A field of golden wheat.
And if thou showest a handful of seed
To a fool,
He will see only that which is before him,
And call them worthless pebbles.
And as the field of the wise man
Giveth forth grain in abundance,
And the field of the fool
Is a harvest only of stones,
So it is with our thoughts.
As the sheaf of golden wheat
Lieth hidden within the tiny kernel,
So is the kingdom of heaven
Hidden within our thoughts.
If they be filled with the
Power, Love and Wisdom
Of the Angels of the Heavenly Father,
So they shall carry us
To the Heavenly Sea.
But if they be stained

With corruption, hatred and ignorance,
They shall chain our feet
To pillars of pain and suffering.
No man can serve two masters;
Neither can evil thoughts abide in a mind
Filled with the Light of the Law.
He who hath found peace with the mind
Hath learned to soar beyond
The Realm of the Angels.
Know this peace with thy mind,
Desire this peace with thy heart,
Fulfill this peace with thy body.

Blessed is the Child of Light
Who is pure in heart,
For he shall see God.
For as the Heavenly Father hath given thee
His holy spirit,
And thy Earthly Mother hath given thee
Her holy body,
So shall ye give love
To all thy brothers.
And thy true brothers are all those
Who do the will of thy Heavenly Father
And thy Earthly Mother.
Let thy love be as the sun
Which shines on all the creatures of the earth,
And does not favor one blade of grass
For another.
And this love shall flow as a fountain
From brother to brother,
And as it is spent,

So shall it be replenished.
For love is eternal.
Love is stronger
Than the currents of deep waters.
Love is stronger than death.
And if a man hath not love,
He doth build a wall between him
And all the creatures of the earth,
And therein doth he dwell
In loneliness and pain.
Or he may become as an angry whirlpool
Which sucks into its depths
All that floats too near.
For the heart is a sea with mighty waves,
And love and wisdom must temper it,
As the warm sun breaks through the clouds
And quiets the restless sea.
He who hath found peace with his brothers
Hath entered the kingdom of Love,
And shall see God face to face.
Know this peace with thy mind,
Desire this peace with thy heart,
Fulfill this peace with thy body.

Blessed is the Child of Light
Who doth build on earth
The kingdom of heaven,
For he shall dwell in both worlds.
Thou shalt follow the Law
Of the Brotherhood,
Which saith that none shall have wealth,
And none shall be poor,

And all shall work together
In the garden of the Brotherhood.
Yet each shall follow his own path,
And each shall commune with his own heart.
For in the Infinite Garden
There are many and diverse flowers:
Who shall say that one is best
Because its color is purple,
Or that one is favored
Because its stalk is long and slender?
Though the brothers
Be of different complexion,
Yet do they all toil
In the vineyard of the Earthly Mother,
And they all do lift their voices together
In praise of the Heavenly Father.
And together they break the holy bread,
And in silence share the holy meal
Of thanksgiving.
There shall be no peace among peoples
Till there be one garden of the brotherhood
Over the earth.
For how can there be peace
When each man pursueth his own gain
And doth sell his soul into slavery?
Thou, Child of Light,
Do ye gather with thy brothers
And then go ye forth
To teach the ways of the Law
To those who would hear.
He who hath found peace
With the brotherhood of man

Hath made himself
The co-worker of God.
Know this peace with thy mind,
Desire this peace with thy heart,
Fulfill this peace with thy body.

Blessed is the Child of Light
Who doth study the Book of the Law,
For he shall be as a candle
In the dark of night,
And an island of truth
In a sea of falsehood.
For know ye, that the written word
Which cometh from God
Is a reflection of the Heavenly Sea,
Even as the bright stars
Reflect the face of heaven.
As the words of the Ancient Ones
Are etched with the hand of God
On the Holy Scrolls,
So is the Law engraved on the hearts
Of the faithful who do study them.
For it was said of old,
That in the beginning there were giants
In the earth,
And mighty men which were of old,
Men of renown.
And the Children of Light
Shall guard and preserve
Their written word,
Lest we become again as beasts,
And know not the Kingdom of the Angels.

Know ye, too,
That only through the written word
Shalt thou find that Law
Which is unwritten,
As the spring which floweth from the ground
Hath a hidden source
In the secret depths beneath the earth.
The written Law
Is the instrument by which
The unwritten Law is understood,
As the mute branch of a tree
Becomes a singing flute
In the hands of the shepherd.
Many there are
Who would stay in the tranquil
Valley of ignorance,
Where children play
And butterflies dance in the sun
For their short hour of life.
But none can tarry there long,
And ahead rise the somber
Mountains of learning.
Many there are
Who fear to cross,
And many there are
Who have fallen bruised and bleeding
From their steep and rugged slopes.
But faith is the guide
Over the gaping chasm,
And perseverance the foothold
In the jagged rocks.
Beyond the icy peaks of struggle

Lies the peace and beauty
Of the Infinite Garden of Knowledge,
Where the meaning of the Law
Is made known to the Children of Light.
Here in the center of its forest
Stands the Tree of Life,
Mystery of mysteries.
He who hath found peace
With the teachings of the Ancients,
Through the light of the mind,
Through the light of nature,
And through the study of the Holy Word,
Hath entered the cloud-filled
Hall of the Ancients,
Where dwelleth the Holy Brotherhood,
Of whom no man may speak.
Know this peace with thy mind,
Desire this peace with thy heart,
Fulfill this peace with thy body.

Blessed is the Child of Light
Who knoweth his Earthly Mother,
For she is the giver of life.
Know that thy Mother is in thee,
And thou art in her.
She bore thee
And she giveth thee life.
She it was who gaveth thee thy body,
And to her shalt thou one day
Give it back again.
Know that the blood which runs in thee
Is born of the blood

Of thy Earthly Mother.
Her blood falls from the clouds,
Leaps up from the womb of the earth,
Babbles in the brooks of the mountains,
Flows wide in the rivers of the plains,
Sleeps in the lakes,
Rages mightily in the tempestuous seas.
Know that the air which thou dost breathe
Is born of the breath
Of thy Earthly Mother.
Her breath is azure
In the heights of the heavens,
Soughs in the tops of the mountains,
Whispers in the leaves of the forest,
Billows over the cornfields,
Slumbers in the deep valleys,
Burns hot in the desert.
Know that the hardness of thy bones
Is born of the bones
Of thy Earthly Mother,
Of the rocks and of the stones.
Know that the tenderness of thy flesh
Is born of the flesh
Of thy Earthly Mother,
She whose flesh waxeth yellow and red
In the fruits of the trees.
The light of thy eyes,
The hearing of thy ears,
These are born
Of the colors and the sounds
Of thy Earthly Mother,
Which doth enclose thee about,

As the waves of the sea enclose a fish,
As the eddying air a bird.
I tell thee in truth,
Man is the Son
Of the Earthly Mother,
And from her did the Son of Man
Receive his whole body,
Even as the body of the newborn babe
Is born of the womb of his mother.
I tell thee truly,
Thou art one with the Earthly Mother;
She is in thee, and thou art in her.
Of her wert thou born,
In her dost thou live,
And to her shalt thou return again.
Keep, therefore, her laws,
For none can live long,
Neither be happy,
But he who honors his Earthly Mother
And keepeth her laws.
For thy breath is her breath,
Thy blood her blood,
Thy bone her bone,
Thy flesh her flesh,
Thy eyes and thy ears
Are her eyes and her ears.
He who hath found peace
With his Earthly Mother
Shall never know death.
Know this peace with thy mind,
Desire this peace with thy heart,
Fulfill this peace with thy body.

Blessed is the Child of Light
Who doth seek his Heavenly Father,
For he shall have eternal life.
He that dwelleth in the secret place
Of the Most High
Shall abide under the shadow
Of the Almighty.
For he shall give his Angels charge over thee,
To keep thee in all thy ways.
Know ye that the Lord hath been
Our dwelling place
In all generations.
Before the mountains were brought forth,
Or ever he had formed
The earth and the world,
Even from everlasting to everlasting,
Hath there been love
Between the Heavenly Father
And his children.
And how shall this love be severed?
From the beginning
Until the ending of time
Doth the holy flame of love
Encircle the heads
Of the Heavenly Father
And the Children of Light:
How then shall this love be extinguished?
For not as a candle doth it burn,
Nor yet as a fire raging in the forest.
Lo, it burneth with the flame
Of Eternal Light,
And that flame cannot be consumed.

Ye that love thy Heavenly Father,
Do ye then his bidding:
Walk ye with his Holy Angels,
And find thy peace with his Holy Law.
For his Law is the entire Law:
Yea, it is the Law of laws.
Through his Law he hath made
The earth and the heavens to be one;
The mountains and the sea
Are his footstools.
With his hands he hath made us
And fashioned us,
And he gaveth us understanding
That we may learn his Law.
He is covered with Light
As with a garment:
He stretcheth out the heavens
Like a curtain.
He maketh the clouds his chariot;
He walketh upon the wings of the wind.
He sendeth the springs into the valleys,
And his breath is in the mighty trees.
In his hand are the deep places of the earth:
The strength of the hills is his also.
The sea is his,
And his hands formed the dry land.
All the heavens declare the Glory of God,
And the firmament showeth his Law.
And to his children
Doth he bequeath his Kingdom,
To those who walk with his Angels,
And find their peace with his Holy Law.

Wouldst thou know more, my children?
How may we speak with our lips
That which cannot be spoken?
It is like a pomegranate eaten by a mute:
How then may he tell of its flavor?
If we say the Heavenly Father
Dwelleth within us,
Then are the heavens ashamed;
If we say he dwelleth without us,
It is falsehood.
The eye which scanneth the far horizon
And the eye which seeth the hearts of men
He maketh as one eye.
He is not manifest,
He is not hidden.
He is not revealed,
Nor is he unrevealed.
My children, there are no words
To tell that which he is!
Only this do we know:
We are his children,
And he is our Father.
He is our God,
And we are the children of his pasture,
And the sheep of his hand.
He who hath found peace
With his Heavenly Father
Hath entered the Sanctuary
Of the Holy Law,
And hath made a covenant with God
Which shall endure forever.
Know this peace with thy mind,

Desire this peace with thy heart,
Fulfill this peace with thy body.
Though heaven and earth may pass away,
Not one letter of the Holy Law
Shall change or pass away.
For in the beginning was the Law,
And the Law was with God,
And the Law was God.
May the Sevenfold Peace
Of the Heavenly Father
Be with thee always.

And Enoch walked with God;
and he was not;
for God took him.

Essene Genesis 5:24

The Law was planted in the garden of the
Brotherhood
to enlighten the heart of man
and to make straight before him
all the ways of true righteousness,
an humble spirit, an even temper,
a freely compassionate nature,
and eternal goodness and understanding and insight,
and mighty wisdom which believes in all God's
works
and a confident trust in His many blessings
and a spirit of knowledge in all things of the Great
Order,
loyal feelings toward all the children of truth,
a radiant purity which loathes everything impure,
a discretion regarding all the hidden things of truth
and secrets of inner knowledge.

from the Manual of Discipline
of the Dead Sea Scrolls

Thou hast made known unto me
Thy deep, mysterious things.
All things exist by Thee
and there is none beside Thee.
By Thy Law

Thou hast directed my heart
that I set my steps straight forward
upon right paths
and walk where Thy presence is.

from the Book of Hymns VII
of the Dead Sea Scrolls

The Law was planted to reward the children of light
with healing and abundant peace,
with long life,
with fruitful seed of everlasting blessings,
with eternal joy
in immortality of eternal Light.

from the Manual of Discipline
of the Dead Sea Scrolls

I thank Thee, Heavenly Father,
because Thou hast put me
at a source of running streams,
at a living spring in a land of drought,
watering an eternal garden of wonders,
the Tree of Life, mystery of mysteries,
growing everlasting branches for eternal planting
to sink their roots into the stream of life
from an eternal source.
And Thou, Heavenly Father,
protect their fruits
with the angels of the day
and of the night
and with flames of eternal Light burning every way.

from the Thanksgiving Psalms
of the Dead Sea Scrolls

I am grateful, Heavenly Father,
for Thou hast raised me to an eternal height
and I walk in the wonders of the plain.
Thou gavest me guidance
to reach Thine eternal company
from the depths of the earth.
Thou hast purified my body
to join the army of the angels of the earth
and my spirit to reach
the congregation of the heavenly angels.
Thou gavest man eternity
to praise at dawn and dusk
Thy works and wonders
in joyful song.

from the Thanksgiving Psalms
of the Dead Sea Scrolls

I will praise Thy works
with songs of Thanksgiving
continually, from period to period,
in the circuits of the day, and in its fixed order;
with the coming of light from its source
and at the turn of evening and the outgoing of light,
at the outgoing of darkness and the coming in of day,
continually,
in all the generations of time.

from the Thanksgiving Psalms
of the Dead Sea Scrolls

May He bless thee with every good,
may He keep thee from all evil
and illumine thy heart with the knowledge of life

and favor thee with eternal wisdom.
And may He give His Sevenfold blessings upon thee
to everlasting Peace.

from the Manual of Discipline
of the Dead Sea Scrolls

With the coming of day
I embrace my Mother,
with the coming of night
I join my Father,
and with the outgoing of evening and morning
I will breathe Their Law,
and I will not interrupt these Communions
until the end of time.

from the Manual of Discipline
of the Dead Sea Scrolls

He assigned to man two spirits with which he
*   should walk.*
They are the spirits of truth and of falsehood,
truth born out of the spring of Light,
falsehood from the well of darkness.
The dominion of all the children of truth
is in the hands of the Angels of Light
so that they walk in the ways of Light.
The spirits of truth and falsehood struggle within
*   the heart of man,*
behaving with wisdom and folly.
And according as a man inherits truth
so will he avoid darkness.
Blessings on all that have cast their lot with the Law,
that walk truthfully in all their ways.

May the Law bless them with all good
and keep them from all evil
and illumine their hearts with insight into the things
of life
and grace them with knowledge of things eternal.

from the Manual of Discipline
of the Dead Sea Scrolls

I have reached the inner vision
and through Thy spirit in me
I have heard Thy wondrous secret.
Through Thy mystic insight
Thou hast caused a spring of knowledge
to well up within me,
a fountain of power,
pouring forth living waters,
a flood of love
and of all-embracing wisdom
like the splendor of eternal Light.

from the Book of Hymns of the Dead Sea Scrolls

FROM THE ESSENE BOOK
OF
THE TEACHER OF RIGHTEOUSNESS

And the Master took himself to the banks of a stream where the people were gathered, those who did hunger after his words. And he blessed them, and asked them whereof they were troubled. And one did speak: "Master, tell us what are those things we should hold of high value, and what are those things we should despise?"

And the Master answered, saying, "All the ills which men suffer are caused by those things without us; for what is within us can never make us suffer. A child dies, a fortune is lost, house and fields burn, and all men are helpless, and they cry out, 'What shall I do now? What shall now befall me? Will this thing come to pass?' All these are the words of those who grieve and rejoice over events which do befall them, events which are not of their doing. But if we do mourn over that which is not in our power, we are as the little child who weeps when the sun leaves the sky. It was said of old, thou shalt not covet any thing that is thy neighbor's; and now I say unto thee, thou shalt not desire any thing which is not in thy power, for only that which is within thee doth belong to thee; and that which is without thee doth belong to another. In this doth happiness lie: to know what is thine, and what is not thine. If thou wouldst have eternal life, hold fast to the eternity within thee, and grasp not at the shadows of the world of men, which hold the seeds of death."

"Is not all that happens without thee, outside of thy power? It is. And thy knowledge of good and evil, is it not within thee? It is. Is it not, then, in thy power, to treat of all which doth come to pass in the light of wisdom and love, instead of sadness and despair? It is. Can any man hinder thee from doing thus? No man can. Then shalt thou not cry out, 'What shall I do? What shall now befall me? Will this thing come to pass?' For whatsoever may come to pass, thou shalt judge it in the light of wisdom and love, and see all things with the eyes of the Angels."

"For to weigh thy happiness according to that which may befall thee, is to live as a slave. And to live according to the Angels which speak within thee, is to be free. Thou shalt live in freedom as a true son of God, and bow thy head only to the commandments of the Holy Law. In this way shalt thou live, that when the Angel of Death cometh for thee, thou canst stretch out thy hands to God, and say, 'The Communions I have received from thee for knowing thy Law and walking in the paths of the Angels, I have not neglected: I have not dishonored thee by my acts: see how I have used the eye which seeth within: have I ever blamed thee? Have I cried out against that which hath befallen me, or desired that it be otherwise? Have I desired to transgress thy Law? That thou hast given me life, I thank thee for what thou hast given me: so long as I have used the things which are thine, I am content: take them back and place them wherever thou mayest choose, for thine are all things, even unto eternity.' "

"Know ye, that no man can serve two masters. Thou canst not wish to have the world's riches, and have also the Kingdom of Heaven. Thou canst not wish to own lands and wield power over men, and have also the Kingdom of Heaven. Wealth, lands and power, these things belong to no man, for they are of the world. But the Kingdom of Heaven is thine forever, for it is within thee. And if thou dost desire and seek after that which doth not belong to thee, then shalt thou surely lose that which is thine. Know ye, for I tell thee truly, that nothing is given nor is it had for nothing. For every thing in the world of men and angels, there is a price. He who would gather wealth and riches must run about, kiss the hands of those he admires not, waste himself with fatigue at other men's doors, say and do many false things, give gifts of gold and silver and sweet oils; all this and more must a man do to gather wealth and favor. And when thou hast achieved it, what then dost thou have? Will this wealth and power secure for thee freedom from fear, a mind at peace, a day spent in the company of the Angels of the Earthly Mother, a night spent in communion with the Angels of the Heavenly Father? Dost thou expect to have for nothing, things so great? When a man hath two masters, either he will hate the one, and love the other; or else he will hold to the one, and despise the other. Ye cannot serve God and also serve the world. Perchance thy well goeth dry, precious oil is spilled, thy house burneth, thy crops wither: but thou dost treat what may befall thee with wisdom and love. Rains again shall fill the well, houses can again be built, new seeds can be sown: all these things shall pass away, and come again, and yet again pass away. But the kingdom of heaven is eternal, and shall not pass away. Do ye not, then, barter that which is eternal, for that which dieth in an hour."

* * *

When men shall ask of thee, to what country dost thou belong, say ye not that thou art of this country or that, for of truth, it is only the poor body which is born in one small corner of this earth. But thou, O Child of Light, belongeth to the Brotherhood which doth encompass all the heavens and beyond, and from thy Heavenly Father hath descended the seeds not only of thy father and grandfather, but of all beings which are generated on the earth. In truth, thou art a son of God, and all men thy brothers: and to have God for thy maker and thy father and guardian, shall not this release us from all sorrow and fear?

Therefore, I say unto thee, take no thought to store up worldly goods, possessions, gold and silver, for these bring only corruption and death. For the greater thy hoard of wealth, the thicker shall be the walls of thy tomb. Open wide the windows of thy soul, and breathe the fresh air of a free man! Why take ye thought for raiment? Consider the lilies of the field, how they grow: they toil not, neither do they spin: and yet I say unto thee, that even Solomon in his glory was not arrayed like one of these. Why take ye thought for nourishment? Consider the gifts of thy Earthly Mother: the ripe fruits of her trees, and the golden grain of her soil. Why take ye thought for house and lands? A man cannot sell to thee that which he doth not own, and he cannot own that which already doth belong to all. This wide earth is thine, and all men are thy brothers. The Angels of the Earthly Mother walk with thee by day, and the Angels of the Heavenly Father guide thee by night, and within thee is the Holy Law. It is not meet for the son of a king to covet a bauble in the gutter. Take thy place, then, at the table of the celebration, and fulfill thy inheritance with honor. For in God we live, and move, and have our being. In truth, we are his sons, and he is our Father.

* * *

He only is free who liveth as he doth desire to live; who is not hindered in his acts, and whose desires attaineth their ends. He who is not restrained is free, but he who can be restrained or hindered, that man is surely a slave. But who is not a slave? That man only who desireth nothing which doth belong to others. And what are those things which belong to thee? My children, only the kingdom of heaven within thee, where the Law of thy Heavenly Father doth dwell, doth belong to thee. The kingdom of heaven is like unto a merchant man, seeking goodly pearls: who, when he had found one pearl of great price, went and sold all that he had, and bought it. And if this one precious pearl be thine forever, why dost thou barter it for pebbles and stones? Know ye, that thy house, thy land, thy sons and daughters, all the joys of fortune and sorrows of tribulation, yea, even that opinion which others do hold of thee, all these things belong to thee not. And if ye then do lust after these things, and hold fast to them, and grieve and exult over them, then in truth thou art a slave, and in slavery wilt thou remain.

My children, let not the things which are not thine cleave unto thee! Let not the world grow unto thee, as the creeping vine groweth fast to the oak, so that thou dost suffer pain when it is torn from thee. Naked camest thou from thy mother's womb, and naked shalt thou return thither. The world giveth and the world taketh away. But no power in heaven or earth can take from thee the Holy Law which doth reside within thee. Thou mayest see thy parents slain, and from thy country mayest thou be driven. Then shalt thou go with cheerful heart to live in another, and look with pity on the slayer of thy parents, knowing that by the deed he doth slay himself. For thou knowest thy true parents, and thou livest secure in thy true country. For thy true parents are thy Heavenly Father and thy Earthly Mother, and thy true country is the Kingdom of Heaven. Death can never separate thee from thy true parents, and from thy true country there is no exile. And within thee, a rock which standeth against all storms, is the Holy Law, thy bulwark and thy salvation.

In the beginning was the Law, and the Law was with God, and the Law was God. The same was in the beginning with God. All things were made by him; and without him was not anything made that was made. In him was life; and the life was the light of men. And the light shineth in the darkness; and the darkness comprehended it not.

From the far place in the desert came the Brothers, to bear witness of the Light, that all men through them might walk in the light of the Holy Law. For the true light doth illumine every man that cometh into the world, but the world knoweth it not. But as many do receive the Law, to them is given the power to become the Sons of God, and to enter the Eternal Sea where standeth the Tree of Life.

And Jesus taught them, saying, Verily, verily, I say unto thee, except a man be born again, he cannot see the Kingdom of Heaven.

And one man said, How can a man be born when he is old? Can he enter a second time into his mother's womb, and be born?

And Jesus answered, Verily, verily, I say unto thee, Except a man be born of the Earthly Mother and the Heavenly Father, and walk with the Angels of the Day and the Night, he cannot enter into the Eternal Kingdom. That which is born of the flesh is flesh; and that which is born of the Spirit is spirit. And the flesh of thy body is born of the Earthly Mother, and the spirit within thee is born of the Heavenly Father. The wind bloweth where it listeth, and thou hearest the sound thereof, but canst not tell whence it cometh. So it is with the Holy Law. All men hear it, but know it not, for from their first breath it is with them. But he who is born again of the Heavenly Father and the Earthly Mother, he shall hear with new ears, and see with new eyes, and the flame of the Holy Law shall be kindled within him.

And one man asked, How can these things be?

Jesus answered and said unto him, Verily, verily, I say unto thee, We speak that we do know, and testify that we have seen;

and ye receive not our witness. For man is born to walk with the Angels, but instead he doth search for jewels in the mud. To him hath the Heavenly Father bestowed his inheritance, that he should build the Kingdom of Heaven on earth, but man hath turned his back on his Father, and doth worship the world and its idols. And this is the condemnation, that light is come into the world, and men loved darkness rather than light, because their deeds were evil. For every one that doeth evil hateth the light, neither cometh to the light. For we are all Sons of God, and in us God is glorified. And the light which shineth around God and his children is the Light of the Holy Law. And he who hateth the light, doth deny his Father and his Mother, who have given him birth.

And one man asked, Master, how can we know the light?

And Jesus answered, Verily, verily, I give unto thee a new commandment: that ye love one another, even as they love thee who work together in the Garden of the Brotherhood. By this shall all men know that ye too are brothers, even as we all are Sons of God.

And one man said, All thy talk is of the brotherhood, yet we cannot all be of the brotherhood. Yet we would worship light and shun darkness, for none there is among us who desireth evil.

And Jesus answered, Let not thy heart be troubled: ye believe in God. Know ye that in our Father's house are many mansions, and our brotherhood is but a dark glass reflecting the Heavenly Brotherhood unto which all creatures of heaven and earth do belong. The brotherhood is the vine, and our Heavenly Father is the husbandman. Every branch in us that beareth not fruit he taketh away: and every branch that beareth fruit, he purgeth it, that it may bring forth more fruit. Abide in us, and we in thee. As the branch cannot bear fruit of itself, except it abide in the vine, no more can ye, except ye abide in the Holy Law, which is the rock upon which our brotherhood stands. He that abideth in the Law, the same bringeth forth much fruit: for without the Law ye can do nothing. If a man abide not in the Law, he is cast forth as a branch, and is withered; and men gather them, and cast them into the fire, and they are burned.

And as the brothers abide in the love one for another, as the Angel of Love doth teach them, so we do ask that ye love one another. Greater love hath no man than this, to teach the Holy Law one to another, and to love each other as oneself. The Heavenly Father is in us, and we are in him, and we do reach out our hands in love and ask that ye be one in us. The glory which he gavest us we do give to thee: that thou mayest be one, even as we are one. For thy Father in Heaven hath loved thee before the foundation of the world.

And in this manner did the Brothers teach the Holy Law to them who would hear it, and it is said they did marvelous things, and healed the sick and afflicted with diverse grasses and wondrous uses of sun and water. And there are also many other things they did, the which, if they should be written every one, even the world itself could not contain the books that should be written. Amen.

FRAGMENTS FROM

THE ESSENE BOOK OF REVELATIONS

Behold, the Angel of Air shall bring him,
And every eye shall see him,
And the brotherhood,
All the vast brotherhood of the earth
Shall raise their voice as one and sing,
Because of him.
Even so, Amen.

I am Alpha and Omega, the beginning and the end;
Which is, which was, and which is to come.

And the voice spoke, and I turned to see
The voice that spoke with me.
And being turned, I saw seven golden candles;
And in the midst of their blazing light
I saw one like unto the Son of Man,
Clothed in white, white as the snow.
And his voice filled the air with the sound of rushing water;
And in his hands were seven stars,
Full of the flaming light of the heavens from whence they came.
And when he spoke, his face was streaming light,
Blazing and golden like a thousand suns.

And he said, "Fear not, I am the first and the last;
I am the beginning and the end.
Write the things which thou hast seen,
And the things which are, and the things which shall be hereafter;
The mystery of the seven stars which fill my hands,
And the seven golden candles, blazing with eternal light.
The seven stars are the Angels of the Heavenly Father,
And the seven candles are the Angels of the Earthly Mother.

And the spirit of man is the flame
Which streams between the starlight and the glowing candle:
A bridge of holy light between heaven and earth.

These things saith he that holdeth seven stars in his hands,
Who walketh in the midst of the flames of seven golden candles.
He that hath an ear, let him hear what the Spirit saith:
"To him that overcometh will I give to eat of the Tree of Life,
That standeth in the midst of the shining Paradise of God."

And then I looked, and, behold,
A door was opened in heaven:
And a voice which sounded from all sides, like a trumpet,
Spoke to me: "Come up hither,
And I will show thee things which must be hereafter."

And immediately I was there, in spirit,
At the threshold of the open door.
And I entered through the open door
Into a sea of blazing light.
And in the midst of the blinding ocean of radiance was a throne;
And on the throne sat one whose face was hidden.
And there was a rainbow round about the throne,
In sight like unto an emerald.
And round about the throne were thirteen seats:
And upon the seats I saw thirteen elders sitting,
Clothed in white raiment;
And their faces were hidden by swirling clouds of light.
And seven lamps of fire burned before the throne,
The fire of the Earthly Mother.
And seven stars of heaven shone before the throne,
The fire of the Heavenly Father.
And before the throne
There was a sea of glass like unto crystal:

And reflected therein
Were all the mountains and valleys and oceans of the earth,
And all the creatures abiding therein.
And the thirteen elders bowed down before the splendor of him
Who sat on the throne, whose face was hidden,
And rivers of light streamed from their hands, one to the other,
And they cried, "Holy, holy, holy,
Lord God Almighty,
Which was, and is, and is to come.
Thou art worthy, O Lord,
To receive glory and honor and power:
For thou hast created all things."

And then I saw in the right hand
Of him that sat on the throne,
Whose face was hidden,
A book written within and on the backside,
Sealed with seven seals.
And I saw an angel proclaiming with a loud voice,
"Who is worthy to open the book,
And to loose the seals thereof?"

And no being in heaven, nor in earth, neither under the earth,
Was able to open the book, neither to look thereon.
And I wept, because the book could not be opened,
Nor was I able to read what there was written.
And one of the elders saith unto me, "Weep not.
Reach out thy hand, and take the book,
Yea, even the book with the seven seals, and open it.
For it was written for thee,
Who art at once the lowest of the low,
And the highest of the high."

And I reached out my hand and touched the book.

And, behold, the cover lifted,
And my hands touched the golden pages,
And my eyes beheld the mystery of the seven seals.

And I beheld, and I heard the voice of many angels
Round about the throne,
And the number of them was ten thousand times ten thousand,
And thousands of thousands, saying with a loud voice,
"All glory, and wisdom, and strength,
And power forever and ever,
To him who shall reveal the Mystery of Mysteries."
And I saw the swirling clouds of golden light
Stretching like a fiery bridge between my hands,
And the hands of the thirteen elders,
And the feet of him who sat on the throne,
Whose face was hidden.

And I opened the first seal.
And I saw, and beheld the Angel of Air.
And between her lips flowed the breath of life,
And she knelt over the earth
And gave to man the winds of Wisdom.
And man breathed in.
And when he breathed out, the sky darkened,
And the sweet air became foul and fetid,
And clouds of evil smoke hung low over all the earth.
And I turned my face away in shame.

And I opened the second seal.
And I saw, and beheld the Angel of Water.
And between her lips flowed the water of life,
And she knelt over the earth
And gave to man an ocean of Love.
And man entered the clear and shining waters.

And when he touched the water, the clear streams darkened,
And the crystal waters became thick with slime,
And the fish lay gasping in the foul blackness,
And all creatures died of thirst.
And I turned my face away in shame.

And I opened the third seal.
And I saw, and beheld the Angel of Sun.
And between her lips flowed the light of life,
And she knelt over the earth
And gave to man the fires of Power.
And the strength of the sun entered the heart of man,
And he took the power, and made with it a false sun,
And, lo, he spread the fires of destruction,
Burning the forests, laying waste the green valleys,
Leaving only charred bones of his brothers.
And I turned my face away in shame.

And I opened the fourth seal.
And I saw, and beheld the Angel of Joy.
And between her lips flowed the music of life,
And she knelt over the earth
And gave to man the song of Peace.
And peace and joy like music
Flowed through the soul of man.
But he heard only the harsh discord of sadness and discontent,
And he lifted up his sword
And cut off the hands of the peacemakers,
And lifted it up once again
And cut off the heads of the singers.
And I turned my face away in shame.

And I opened the fifth seal.
And I saw, and beheld the Angel of Life.

And between her lips
Flowed the holy alliance between God and Man,
And she knelt over the earth
And gave to man the gift of Creation.
And man created a sickle of iron in the shape of a serpent,
And the harvest he reaped was hunger and death.
And I turned my face away in shame.

And I opened the sixth seal.
And I saw, and beheld the Angel of Earth.
And between her lips flowed the river of Eternal Life,
And she knelt over the earth
And gave to man the secret of eternity,
And told him to open his eyes
And behold the mysterious Tree of Life in the Endless Sea.
But man lifted his hand and put out his own eyes,
And said there was no eternity.
And I turned my face away in shame.

And I opened the seventh seal.
And I saw, and beheld the Angel of the Earthly Mother.
And she brought with her a message of blazing light
From the throne of the Heavenly Father.
And this message was for the ears of man alone,
He who walks between earth and heaven.
And into the ear of man was whispered the message.
And he did not hear.
But I did not turn away my face in shame.
Lo, I reached forth my hand to the wings of the angel,
And I turned my voice to heaven, saying,
"Tell me the message. For I would eat of the fruit
Of the Tree of Life that grows in the Sea of Eternity."
And the angel looked upon me with great sadness,

And there was silence in heaven.
And then I heard a voice, which was like unto the voice
Which sounded like a trumpet, saying,
"O Man, wouldst thou look upon the evil thou hast wrought,
When thou didst turn thy face away from the throne of God,
When thou didst not make use of the gifts
Of the seven Angels of the Earthly Mother
And the seven Angels of the Heavenly Father?
And a terrible pain seized me as I felt within me
The souls of all those who had blinded themselves,
So as to see only their own desires of the flesh.
And I saw the seven angels which stood before God;
And to them were given seven trumpets.
And another angel came and stood at the altar,
Having a golden censer;
And there was given unto him much incense,
That he should offer it with the prayers of all the angels
Upon the golden altar which was before the throne.
And the smoke of the incense ascended up before God
Out of the angel's hand.
And the angel took the censer,
And filled it with the fire of the altar,
And cast it into the earth,
And there were voices and thunderings,
And lightnings, and earthquakes.
And the seven angels which had the seven trumpets
Prepared themselves to sound.

The first angel sounded,
And there followed hail and fire mingled with blood,
And they were cast upon the earth:
And the green forests and trees were burnt up,
And all green grass shriveled to cinders.

And the second angel sounded,
And as it were a great mountain burning with fire
Was cast into the sea:
And blood rose from the earth as a vapor.

And the fourth angel sounded,
And lo, there was a great earthquake;
And the sun became as black as sackcloth of hair,
And the moon became as blood.

And the fifth angel sounded,
And the stars of heaven fell unto the earth,
Even as a fig tree casteth her untimely figs,
When she is shaken of a mighty wind.

And the sixth angel sounded,
And the heaven departed as a scroll when it is rolled together.
And over the whole earth there was not one tree,
Nor one flower, nor one blade of grass.
And I stood on the earth,
And my feet sank into the soil, soft and thick with blood,
Stretching as far as the eye could see.
And over all the earth was silence.

And the seventh angel sounded.
And I saw a mighty being come down from heaven,
Clothed with a cloud:
And a rainbow was upon his head,
And his face was as it were the sun,
And his feet were pillars of fire.
And he had in his hand a book open:
And he set his right foot upon the sea, and his left on the earth,
And he cried with a loud voice, which was wondrous to hear:
"O Man, wouldst thou have this vision come to pass?"

And I answered, "Thou knowest, O Holy One,
That I would do anything
That these terrible things might not come to pass."

And he spoke: "Man has created these powers of destruction.
He has wrought them from his own mind.
He has turned his face away
From the Angels of the Heavenly Father and the Earthly Mother,
And he has fashioned his own destruction."

And I spoke: "Then is there no hope, bright angel?"
And a blazing light streamed like a river from his hands
As he answered, "There is always hope,
O thou for whom heaven and earth were created."

And then the angel,
He who stood upon the sea and upon the earth,
Lifted up his hand to heaven,
And swore by him that liveth for ever and ever,
Who created heaven, and the things that therein are,
And the earth, and the things that therein are,
And the sea, and the things which are therein,
That there should be time no longer:
But in the days of the voice of the seventh angel,
When he shall begin to sound,
The mystery of God should be revealed to those
Who have eaten from the Tree of Life

Which standeth for ever in the Eternal Sea.
And the voice spoke again, saying:
"Go, and take the book which is open in the hand of the angel
Which standeth upon the sea and upon the earth."
And I went unto the angel, and said unto him,
"Give me the book,
For I would eat from the Tree of Life

Which standeth in the middle of the Eternal Sea."
And the angel gave to me the book,
And I opened the book, and I read therein
What had always been, what was now,
And what would come to pass.

I saw the holocaust which would engulf the earth,
And the great destruction
Which would drown all her people in oceans of blood.
And I saw too the eternity of man
And the endless forgiveness of the Almighty.
The souls of men were as blank pages in the book,
Always ready for a new song to be there inscribed.

And I lifted up my face
To the seven Angels of the Earthly Mother
And the seven Angels of the Heavenly Father,
And I felt my feet touching the holy brow of the Earthly Mother,
And my fingers touching the holy feet of the Heavenly Father,
And I uttered a hymn of Thanksgiving:

> *I thank thee, Heavenly Father,*
> *Because thou hast put me at a source of running streams,*
> *At a living spring in a land of drought,*
> *Watering an eternal garden of wonders,*
> *The Tree of Life, Mystery of Mysteries,*
> *Growing everlasting branches for eternal planting*
> *To sink their roots into the stream of life*
> *From an eternal source.*
> *And thou, Heavenly Father,*
> *Protect their fruits*
> *With the Angels of the day and of the night*
> *And with flames of Eternal Light burning every way.*

But again the voice spoke,

And again my eyes were drawn away
From the splendors of the realm of light.
"Heed thou, O Man!
Thou mayest step on the right path
And walk in the presence of the Angels.
Thou mayest sing of the Earthly Mother by day
And of the Heavenly Father by night,
And through thy being may course the golden stream of the Law.
But wouldst thou leave thy brothers
To plunge through the gaping chasm of blood,
As the pain-wracked earth shudders and groans
Under her chains of stone?
Canst thou drink of the cup of eternal life,
When thy brothers die of thirst?

And my heart was heavy with compassion,
And I looked, and lo,
There appeared a great wonder in heaven:
A woman clothed with the sun, and the moon under her feet,
And upon her head a crown of seven stars.
And I knew she was the source of running streams
And the Mother of the Forests.

And I stood upon the sand of the sea,
And saw a beast rise up out of the sea,
And from his nostrils wafted foul and loathsome air,
And where he rose from the sea the clear waters turned to slime,
And his body was covered with black and steaming stone.
And the woman clothed with the sun
Reached out her arms to the beast,
And the beast drew near and embraced her.
And lo, her skin of pearl withered beneath his foul breath,
And her back was broken by his arms of crushing rock,

And with tears of blood she sank into the pool of slime.
And from the mouth of the beast there poured armies of men,
Brandishing swords and fighting, one with the other.
And they fought with a terrible anger,
And they cut off their own limbs and clawed out their eyes,
Until they fell into the pit of slime,
Screaming in agony and pain.

And I stepped to the edge of the pool and reached down my hand,
And I could see the swirling maelstrom of blood,
And the men therein, trapped like flies in a web.
And I spoke in a loud voice, saying,
"Brothers, drop thy swords and take hold of my hand.
Leave off this defiling and desecration of she
Who hath given thee birth,
And he who hath given thee thy inheritance.
For thy days of buying and selling are over,
And over, too, thy days of hunting and killing.
For he that leadeth into captivity shall go into captivity,
And he that killeth by the sword must be killed with the sword.
And the merchants of the earth shall weep and mourn,
For no man buyeth thy merchandise any more:
The merchants of gold, and silver, and precious stones,
And of pearls, and fine linen, and purple, and silk, and scarlet,
And marble and beasts, and sheep and horses,
And chariots and slaves and souls of men,
All these things can ye not buy and sell,
For all is buried in a sea of blood
Because thou hast turned thy back on thy father and mother,
And worshipped the beast who would build a paradise of stone.
Drop thy swords, my brothers, and take hold of my hand.

And as our fingers clasped,

I saw in the distance a great city,
White and shining on the far horizon, glowing alabaster.
And there were voices, and thunders, and lightnings,
And there was a great earthquake,
Such as was not since men were upon the earth,
So mighty an earthquake, and so great.
And the great city was divided into three parts,
And the cities of the nations fell:
And the great city came in remembrance before God,
To give unto her the cup of the wine
Of the fierceness of his wrath.
And every island fled away, and the mountains were not found.
And there fell upon men a great hail out of heaven,
Every stone about the weight of a talent.
And a mighty angel took up a stone like a great millstone,
And cast it into the sea, saying,
"Thus with violence shall the great city be thrown down,
And shall be found no more at all.
And the voice of harpers, and musicians, and of pipers,
And of singers, and trumpeters,
Shall be heard no more at all in thee;
And no craftsman, of whatsoever craft he be,
Shall be found any more in thee;
And the sound of a millstone shall be heard
No more at all in thee.
And the light of a candle shall shine
No more at all in thee;
And the voice of the bridegroom and of the bride shall be heard
No more at all in thee:
For thy merchants were the great men of the earth;
For by thy sorceries were all nations deceived.
And in her was found the blood of prophets, and of saints,

And of all that were slain upon the earth."

And my brothers laid hold of my hand,
And they struggled out of the pool of slime
And stood bewildered on the sea of sand,
And skies opened and washed their naked bodies with rain.
And I heard a voice from heaven, as the voice of many waters,
And as the voice of a great thunder:
And I heard the voice of harpers harping with their harps.
And they sung as it were a new song before the throne.

And I saw another angel fly in the midst of heaven,
Having the songs of day and night
And the everlasting gospel to preach unto them
That dwell on the earth,
Unto them that have climbed from the pit of slime
And stand naked and washed by the rain before the throne.
And the angel cried, "Fear God, and give glory to him;
For the hour of his judgment is come:
And worship him that made heaven, and earth,
And the sea, and the fountains of waters."

And I saw heaven open, and beheld a white horse;
And he that sat upon him was called Faithful and True,
And in Righteousness he doth judge.
His eyes were as a flame of fire,
And on his head were many crowns,
And he was cloaked in blazing light
And his feet were bare.
And his name is called the Word of God.
And the Holy Brotherhood followed him upon white horses,
Clothed in fine linen, white and clean.
And they entered the eternal Infinite Garden,
In whose midst stood the Tree of Life.

And the rain-washed naked throngs came before them,
Trembling to receive their judgment.
For their sins were many, and they had defiled the earth,
Yea, they had destroyed the creatures of the land and sea,
Poisoned the ground, fouled the air,
And buried alive the Mother who had given them birth.

But I saw not what befell them, for my vision changed,
And I saw a new heaven and a new earth:
For the first heaven and the first earth were passed away;
And there was no more sea.
And I saw the holy city of the Brotherhood
Coming down from God out of heaven,
Prepared as a bride adorned for her husband.
And I heard a great voice out of heaven saying,
"Lo, the mountain of the Lord's house
Is established in the top of the mountains
And is exalted above the hills;
And all people shall flow unto it.
Come ye, and let us go up to the mountain of the Lord,
To the house of God;
And he will teach us of his ways,
And we will walk in his paths:
For out of the Holy Brotherhood shall go forth the Law.
Behold, the tabernacle of God is with men,
And he will dwell with them, and they shall be his people,
And God himself shall be with them, and be their God.
And God shall wipe away all tears from their eyes;
And there shall be no more death,
Neither sorrow, nor crying,
Neither shall there be any more pain:
For the former things are passed away.

Those who made war shall beat their swords into plowshares,
And their spears into pruninghooks:
Nation shall not lift up sword against nation,
Neither shall they learn war any more:
For the former things are passed away."

And he spoke again: "Behold, I make all things new.
I am Alpha and Omega, the beginning and the end.
I will give unto him that is athirst
Of the fountain of the water of life freely.
He that overcometh shall inherit all things,
And I will be his God, and he shall be my son.
But the fearful, and unbelieving,
And the abominable, and murderers, and all liars,
Shall dig their own pit which burneth with fire and brimstone."

And again my vision changed,
And I heard the voices of the Holy Brotherhood raised in song,
Saying, "Come ye, and let us walk in the light of the Law."
And I saw the holy city,
And the Brothers were streaming unto it.
And the city had no need of the sun,
Neither of the moon, to shine in it:
For the glory of God did lighten it.
And I saw the pure river of the Water of Life,
Clear as crystal, proceeding out of the throne of God.
And in the midst of the river stood the Tree of Life,
Which bore fourteen manner of fruits,
And yielded her fruit to those who would eat of it,
And the leaves of the tree were for the healing of the nations.
And there shall be no night there;
And they need no candle, neither light of the sun,
For the Lord God giveth them light:

And they shall reign for ever and ever.

> I have reached the inner vision
> And through thy spirit in me
> I have heard thy wondrous secret.
> Through thy mystic insight
> Thou hast caused a spring of knowledge
> To well up within me,
> A fountain of power, pouring forth living waters;
> A flood of love and of all-embracing wisdom
> Like the splendor of Eternal Light.

HEBREW TEXTS OF THE ESSENE GOSPEL OF PEACE

ואז באו חולים ובעלי-מום רבים אל ישוע ויהלו פניו לאמור: "אכן
אם גלויות לפניך כל מצפונותנו, הגד נא לנו – על שום מה באונו כל הנגעים
הקשים הללו? מדוע אין אנו ככל שאר האדם? אדוננו – רפא נא לנו למען
נהיה גם אנחנו איתנים ולא נוסיף לדאבה עוד. אכן ידענו אשר יש בכחך
לרפא כל חלי וכל מדווה. אנא, הושיענו מיד השטן וממכותיו בי עצמו ורבו.
רבנו, רחם נא עלינו.

ויען ישוע ויאמר: "אשריכט כי צמאתם לדבר אמת; הנה אני מכלכלכם
בחכמה ודעת. הלוא טוב בי דפקתם – הנה ידעתם לנקיש את דלתות החיים.
אשריכם בי חשברו מעליכם את כבלי השטן, ותביאתם אל מלכת המלאכים אשר
לאמנו; מקרוש שם כחו של השטן לא יוכל לפרוץ". ויתמהו מאד לדבריו וישאלוהו
לאמור: "מי היא אמנו, ואיזה המה מלכיה, והיה מקום ממלכוה?" – "אמכם
היא בקרבכם ואתם – בה. היא הרחה אתכם והיא המעניקה לכם חיים. היא היתה
אשר נתנה לכם את גופכם, ויום יבוא כאשר השב תשיבו לה את גופכם בחזרה.
אשריכם שהנכם באים לדעת אותה ואת מלכותה. והיה אם תקבילו פני מלאכי
אמכם וחלכו בחוקותיה, באמונה אני אומר לכם – זה אשר יקיים דברים אלה
לא יוסיף לראות חלי לעולם. באשר כחה של אמנו עולם מעל לכל. הוא המדביר
את השטן ומכלה את מלכותו; הוא החולש על גופכם ועל כל חי."

"כי הדם הנוזל בעורקינו הוא דמה של אמנו-אדמה. דמה יורד מן
העבים; מזנק מרחם האדמה, מטפטף בערוצי הנהרות; זורם בשביקי הנהרות אשר
בטפלה; מנשב בזגמים ונוגע במעברי חהוט רבה.

"האויר שאנו נושמים אף הוא בא ממצב רוחה של אמנו אדמה; גלום הוא
מהכלת השוקים; שורק ברום ההרים, מלחש בעלות החורש ולוחש בין שבלי הקמה
רוגע בחיק הגיאיות ולוהט במרחבי הישימון. קשיות עצמותינו נוצרה מעצמות
אמנו-אדמה מסלעיה ואבניה. מזדקרים המה במעמיקיהם אל מול פני השמים
במרומי ההרים; נדמים המה לנפלים אשר נרדמו בשעוליהם כפטלי ענק אשר
הוצבו בשמטה המדבר והצפנו עמוק בכליות האדמה. רכות בשרנו נוצרה מבשר
האדמה העולה צח ואדום בפרות האילנות ומצמחנו סבין קפלי השדות.

"בני מעינו באו לנו מתוך כליות אמנו-אדמה והם מוצצנים מראייתנו
בבי שמוצצנים מעמקי האדמה. מאור עינינו ומשמע אזנינו אף המה נובעים
מתוך גוונים וקולותיה של אמנו-אדמה המשפיעים אותנו סביב כאשר יציפו גלי
הים את הדגה, ומערבלי האויר את צרכי כנף.

"באמת ובאמונה אני אומר לכם – האדם הוא בנה של האם-אדמה וממנה
מקבל בן-האדם את כל יצורי גון כאשר יקבל הילוד בצאתו מרחם אמו. ואמנם
אני אומר לכם: אתם ואמכם אחת היא – אתם בה והיא בכם. ממנה יצאתם, בה
הנכם חיים ואליה תשובון. שמרו איפוא חוקותיה, כי אכן לא יאריך אדם
ימים אף לא יהי מאושר אלא אם כן יכבד את האמא-אדמה וימלא אחר מצוותיה.
כי נשימתכם היא נשימתה, דמכם הוא דמה, עצמותיכם, בשרכם –
בשרה, מעיכם – מעיה, עיניכם ואזניכם – עיניה ואזניה.

"באמונה אני אומר לכם, אם חטאו לבקיום אחד מהכללים האלה, אם
תנזקו רק אחד מכל אברי גופכם, הן תחבדו ברוב מחלוחיכם הקשים ובכי וחרוק
שנים יהיו זה מנת חלקכם. אם לא תלכו בחוקות אמכם, מגיד אני לכם, שום
תחבולה לא תמלטכם מזרועות המות. ורק זה אשר דבק בחוקות אמו – אף אמו
תדבק בו. היא תעלה ארוכה לכל מדוויו ולא ישוב לחולות עוד, והיא שתחון לו
אריכות ימים ותגן עליו מכל פגע; מאש וסמים ומהכשת שרף... כי אמכם –
יולדתכם היא המעניקה לכם חיים, היא שפרסה לכם מגופה ושום אחר זולתה
לא ירפאכם. אשרי היא אוהב הורתו ונח שלו בחיקה. כי אמכם אוהבתכם
היא, אף אם אתם מניחם לה עורף, ומה גם כאשר הנכם שבים אליה מחדש? באמונה
אני אומר לכם – רבה, מה רבה היא אהבתה אליכם, גדולה ועצומה היא מענק-
ההרים, עמוקה מעני ים. ואת אלה האוהבים אותה לא תשבוק לעולם. כהגן
התרנגלת על אפרוחיה והלביאה על גוריה וכאם על פרי בטנה – כן מגינה
אמא-אדמה על בן-האדם מכל רעה ופגע.

"וגמנם אני אומר לכם - סכנות ופורענויות לאין ספור אורבות לבן-
האדם. בעל-זבוב אביר כל השדים, מקור כל הרעה, הוא אשר פרש את רשתו
בגופות בני האדם. הוא מלאך השאול השולט על כל מחלה, ובחמדו לו לצון
מפחה הוא את בני האדם וטומן להם פח. עשר ועצמה הוא מבטיח להם, וארמונות
פאר ומדי זהב וכסף וקהל רב מורתחים - הנה את כל אלה! - כן הוא עבטיחם
חיי כבוד ותהלה,פריצות והוללות, זנות ונאפופים ושתיה לשכרה זחיים של
בטלה ורפס מעשה כל הימים. כן הוא מפחה כל איש ועץ לפי חולשתו. והיה
כאשר בני האדם יהפכו להיות לעובדים לכל אלו החובבות והפגולים, אזי
מקבל הוא את שלומיו בנשלו אותם משפע הטובה אשר העניקה להם אמא-אדמה.
שולל מהם או נשימתקת, או דמם, את מיהרם,עיניהם ואזניהם, ונשימם
בן האדם נעשית קצרה וחנוקה, מעונה וסרוחה, כנשימה החיות הטמאות, ודמו
מתעבה ובכאביש כימי המדמנה עד שהוא נצמב ומשחיר כזפלת שאול, ועצמותיו
הוסכבת נוקטות ונכות,ונמקות מתוכן עד התמנפץ כהמנפץ האבן בנפלה על
סדן סלע, ובשרו נעשה שמן ובצקי, מעלה כיבים וטורטות לסוי ולמיאוס,
עד כי נרקב ורוטטש.

"ומעיו נמלאים בזוהמה רירית, ורימה ותולעה פרות ורבות בהן עד לזעוה,
ועיני האדם תכהינה ועולמו יחשך עליו, ואף אזניו תאטמנה כאשר ידם הקול
בקבר, עד כי יספו יתמו חיי האנוש החטוף. יען אשר לא שמר את חוקות אמו
והוסיף חטא על פשע, על כן תשללנה ממנו כל מתנותיה של אמא-אדמה; הנשמה
הדם,ועצמות, הבשר, המים, העינים, והאזנים, ואחרי ככלות הכל - גם
החיים עצמם, אשר בהם אמא-אדם הכשירה את גופו.

"והיה אם הבן ההועה נחם על חטאיו ושב מדרכו הרעה אל אמא-אדמה,ומלא
ימלא אור כל חוקותיה, ומלט עצמו מיד השטן בעמדו בפני פתוייו - או
אז חשוב ותקבלנו אמא-אדמה באהבה וברחמים ותשלו לו את מלאכיה לשרתו.
באמונה אני אומר לכם - כי בה בשעה שבן-האדם יעמד בפני פתויי השטן
השוכן בקרבו ולא יעשה את רצונו - בה בשעה ימצאו מלאכי האם שם מוכנים
לשרתו בכל כחם וישאדו עד אם הוציאוהו כליל מתחת שלטון השטן.

"בשבר שום אדם אינו יכול לעבוד לשני בעלים. או כי ישרת את בעל-
זבוב ועדיו, או ישרת את אמא-אדמה ומלאכיה. או ישרת את החיים או את
המות. באמונה אני אומר לכם: אשרי אלה ההולכים בחוקות החיים ואינם
תועים בדרכי האבדון. כי בהם יעלו כחות החיים כפורחת, ויד החלאים
שוב לא תשיגם."

ויהיו כל המקיפים שומו מאזיניו לדבריו בהתפעלות כי דברו שפע עוז
רב, והוא הורה אותם אחרה לגמרי מכפי שלמדו הכהנים והחכמים. ואף כי
היתה זו עת השקיעה המה לא נפרדו ללכת איש לביתו אך ישבו סביב ישוע
וישאלוהו לאמר: "אדוננו, מה המה חוקי החיים? נא השאר, עמנו עוד מעט
ולמדנו. חפצים אנו לשמע את לקחך למען נרפא והיינו תמימי-דרך;"

וישוע ישב בינתם ויאמר: "באמונה אני אומר לכם - לא יהיה
אדם מאושר אלא אם כן יקיים את החוק." ויענו ויאמרו החכמים: "אנו
מקיימים כלנו את מצוותיו של משה המחוקק, כפי שהמה כתובים בכתבי הקדש".

וישוע אמר: "אל תבקשו את החוק בכתבי הקדש. באשר החוק הוא החיים
עצמם בעוד הכותבים - מות והמה. באמונה אני אומר לכם: משה לא קבל מה'
את החוקים בכתב כי אם באמצעות השם המפורש. החוק הוא השם המפורש מאת
אלהים חיים אל נביאים חיים למען נתשיח חיים. בכל דבר אשר בו חיים
חתום בו גם החוק. השמים ובדגה הים. אך בעיקר בקשוהו בקרבכם אתו. כי באמונה אני אומר
לכם - קרובים הדברים החיים לאלהים יותר משקרובה התורה נטולת החיים.
כי הלא כן ברא ה' את החיים ואת כל חי, על מנת שיוכלו על ידי השם,
המפורש - להורות לאדם את חוקיו של אלהי אמת. ה' לא חרת את חוקיו
על דפי ספרים כי אם בלבבכם וברוחכם. מצויים המה בנשמתכם,בדמכם
ועצמותיכם; בבשרכם,מעיכם,עיניכם,אזניכם ובכל חלק זעיר אשר בגופכם.
נוכחים הם באויר,במים,באדמה,בצומח, בקרני השמש,במעמקי תהום ובגבהי-
מרומים. כל אלה דוברים אליכם למען תבינו את דברי אלהיו חייו ואת
רצונו. אך אתם עוצמים עיניכם למען לא תשמעון; אמת אני אומר לכם
כי כתבי-הקדש הם מעשי ידי אדם בעוד החיים וכל צבאם הם יצורי אלהינו.
אכן, מדוע איפוא, אינכם שומעים את דבר ה' הכתובים למען יצוריו ומדוע
מתעקמים אתם בכתבי-הקדש שהם יצורי כפיו של האדם?

"איכה נוכל לקרוא את חוקי אלוה בלעדי התורה? היכן הם כתובים?
קראם נא לפנינו מתוך מקורן האחר – אין אנו מכירים כל מקור אחר זולתי
התורה, אותה ירשנו מאבותינו."

ויען ישוע: "בין לא תבינו את דבר החיים באשר בני מות הנכם. המחשבה
המעילה על ראייתכם ואזניכם אסמו מטמוע. כי אני אומר לכם – מה בצע לכם
תעיינו באותיות התורה המחות אם בעשיכם אתם מתכחשים לזה אשר נתן לכם
את התורה. באמונה אני אומר לכם – לא במעשיכם שרוי ה' וחוקותיו. אלה
אינם בנמצא לא בזלילה וסביאה, אף לא בחיי תאוה ופריצות ורדיפה אחר
העושר, אף לא בשנאת אויביכם, באשר כל הדברים האלה רחוקים המה מאלהי
אמת ומלמעלין, כי באיש הם מלכות החושך ומדון כל הפורענויות, ואת כל
אלה הדברים נושאים הנכם בקרבכם,כי על כן לא יחדרו בכם דבר ה' ועצמתו
באשר כל דבר וכל דבר וועצה מצאו להם משכן בגופכם ובנשמתכם. אפס
אם תבקשו כי דברי אלהים חיים ועצמתו יבואו בכם, אל תחמאו את גופכם
ונשמתכם. כי הגוף הוא המשכן לרוח והרוח הלוא הוא משכנו של ה', טהרו
איפוא את המקדש למען חבוא בו השכינה ותהפוש את מקומה הראוי לה.

"המלטו איפוא,אל חוות כנפי השכינה מנכלי השטן המעמידכם בנסיון בגוף
וברוח. חדשו עצמכם וצומו – באמונה אני אומר לכם כי את השטן וכפפותיו
אפשר להרחיק רק בכח הצום התפלה והחשובה. לכו איפוא,וצומו לכם בדד לבל
ידע איש על צומכם. האל החי. הוא לבדו ירואנו וגדול יהיה שכרכם. צומו
איפוא, עד אשר בעל-זבוב וכל רעוניו יסתלקו מעליכם וכל המלאבים אשר
לאמנו אדמה יבואו וישרתוכם. כי אמנם אני אומר לכם: אם אינכם צמים –
לעולם לא תהיו משוחררים מכחו של השטן ומכל החליים הטלוחים מאת השטן.
צומו והתפללו ביראה בצפרתכם ליועע אל חי ורפואתו ובעת צומכם ורחקתם
מבני האדם ובקשו את מלכיו אמנו, כי – יגעתם ומצאתם. צאו ובקשו אחר
האויר הצח אשר בשדה וביער מקום שם תפגשו במלאך האויר. שלו נעליכם
מעל רגליכם והסירו כסותכם ותנו למלאך האויר לחבק כל גופכם בכנפיו וזה
שאפו ארוכות ועמוקות לעען יבוא מלאך האויר לקרבכם. באמונה אני אומר
לכם: מלאך יסרט מתוך גופכם את כל הטומאה אשר החליאתו מלבר ומלגו.
וכך יועלו ויצאו מקרבכם כל דבר פגול וצחנה כאשר יעלה חמרות העשן
ויאבדו בים האויר. כי באמת אני אומר לכם: קדוש הוא מלאך האויר המטהר
כל דבר שמא והופך כל דבר מצחין לריח ניחוח. לא יתיצב אדם לפני ה'
עד אם יורשה לעשות כן מאת מלאך האויר, ואמנם הכל צריכים להולד מחדש
באמצעות האויר והאמת. באשר גופכם נושם את האויר של אמכם-אדמה,ורוחכם
נושמת את האמת של אביכם שבשמים.

"לאחר מלאך האויר בקשו את מלאך המים. שלו נעליכם וכסותכם מעליכם
ותנו למלאך המים להציף את גופכם. הפקירו את כל עצמכם לחבוק זרועותיו
וכאשר הנכם מזעזעים את האויר בנשימתכם כן תזעזעו את המים באברי גופכם.
באמונה אני אומר לכם: מלאך המים יסרש מקרבכם את זוהמה אשר הוליאה את
גופכם מלבר ומלגו, וכל דבר שמא וצוחן יצוף ויעלה מתוככם כאשר תעלה
הזוהמה מן הבגדים הצואים בהכבסם במימי הנהר ותתלש עם הזרם. באמונה
אני אומר לכם, קדוש הוא מלאך המים המטהר כל דבר שמא והופך כל דבר
מצחין לריח ניחוח. לא יתיצב אדם לפני ה' עד אם יורשה לעשות כן מאת
מלאך המים. באמת ובתפלים – הכל צריכים להתחדש במים ובאמת, באשר גופכם
טובל בנהר-החיים עלי אדמות, ורוחכם – בנהר חיי-עולם. כי דמכם בא
לכם מאמנו-אדמה, והאמת – מאביכם שבשמים. אל נא תחשוב כי די
לכם בלפף מלאך המים את גופכם מבחוץ. באמונה אני אומר לכם – הטומאה
שבתוככם גדולה רב-יתר מן הטומאה החיצונית. זה המטהר את עצמו מלבר
ומלגו נא נר שמא דומה למצבה הצבועה לתפארה מבחוץ ומסתירה חחזיה
סוחאה עד לזעוה. על כן באמונה אני אומר לכם, חנו למלאך המים ושפפכם
גם מבפנים, לעען חנוקו מכל טומאתכם הנושנים, והפכתם להיות טהורים גם
בתוככם, כאשר יטהר הקצה המפפז באור השמש.

"שלו לכם איפוא ,אחד מן הקשושים, על גבעולו חלול, באורך קומת
אדם, הריקוהו מתוככו, מלאוהו במי-נחל שהפשרו בטמש, ותלוהו בענף האילן.
לאחר מכן כרעו על ברכיכם מלפני מלאך המים ותנו את קצה הגבעול החלול
בפי הטבעת למען יבואו המים הקלוחים מתוך קצהו הצר של הקשו בחלק
גופכם התחתון, ושטפו את קרביכם. לאחר מכן חסארו כורעים על ברכיכם

מול מלאך המים והתפללתם לאל חי כי יסלח לכם את עוונותיכם הנותנים.
כן תתפללו למלאך המים שיטהרכם מכל זוהמה וחלי. ולאחד מכן חניכי למים
שיבלטו מגופכם על מנת שיוטפו מבפנים, את כל דבר פגול ומצחין מסל השטן.
אז תראו בעיניכם ובאפכם תריחו את זו שיצאת מן החלאה והטומאה אשר זהמו את מקדש
גופכם, וכל החטאים אשר שכנו בגופכם ועינוכם ברוב מכאובים ויסורים.

באמת אני אומר לכט: הטבילה במים תפדה אתכם מכל אלה. חדשו את טבילתכם
במים בכל ימי צומכם – עד היום בו תבחינו כי המים היוצאים מגופכם צחים
הם כקצף הנחל. אזי בואו בזרמת הנחל ושם בזרועות מלאך העים חנו תודה
לאל כי הוא שחררכם מכל חטאיכם. וטבילה זו בידי מלאך המים תהא
כלידה מחדש לחיים חדשים. באשר עיניכם יטובו לראות וראזניכם ישבו
לשמוע. אל תוסיפו איפוא, לחטוא לאחר הטבילה, למען ישכנו בכם לנצח
מלאכי האויר והמים, וישרתונכם עדי עד. והיה אם יותר בכם שמץ מחטאיכם
הנושנים ומן הפגולים – בקשו אחרי מלאך אור השמש. שלו נעליכם וכסותכם
מעליכם ותנו לאור השמש ללפף גופכם סביב. אחר וטאפו ארוכות ועמוקות
למען יחדור מלאך אור-השמש לתוככם. ומלאך אור-השמש יכלה מקרבכם כל דבר
טומאה וכל דבר מצחין אשר אילחו את גופכם מבר ומלגו. וכל הטומאה
והבחנה תעלה-תעלה מעליכם כאשר תפוג השכמה הליל שלאני זוהר השמש העולה.
כי באמונה אני אומר לכם: קדוש הוא מלאך-אור-השמש המטהר כל טומאה והופך
כל צחנה לריח-ניחוח. לא יתיצב שום אדם מלפני ה' עד אם יורשה לעשות
כן מאת מלאך-אור-השמש. ואמנם הכל צריכים להתחדש בשמש ובאמת באשר
גופכם טובל בזיו הזוהם של אמא-אדמה ורווחכם – בזיו האמת של האל של שמים.

"מלאכי האויר, המים, ואור השמש אחים המה. הם נתנו לבן-האדם למען
ישרתוהו ולמען יומיד וילך מן האחד אצל משנהו.
"קדוש הוא איפוא, גם חבוקם. בני אמא-אדמה. בני אמא-אדמה המה ללא-הפרד על כן
אל נא תבדילו בין אלה אשר ארץ ושמים אחדום. יאמצוכם איבוא, שלשת
האחים האלה יום-יום וישבו עמכם בעתות צומכם.

"כי אכן, אני אומר לכם: כחות השדים וכל החטאים והתועבות עד מהרה
יסולקו מאותו גוף החבוק על ידי אלה שלשת שלחי המלאכים. כאשר ינוטו הגנבים
מבית זנוח עם שובו של בעליו – האחד מבעד לחתו ומשנהו מבעד לחלון
והשלישי מבעד לגג, איש-איש מהעקוף בו והיה מצוי בדרך המפלט הנגלה לו –
כן ינוסו מקרבכם כל שדי-השחת והחטאים והתועבות והחלאים אשר טמאו לעבר
את מקדש גופכם. אזי יבואו מלאכי אמא-אדמה לאור קרביכם ויכשירום כאשר
יוכשר ההיכל בטרם יבואו אדוניו לשכון בו מחדש. כל הריחות הרעים יונסו
אזי בחפזו דרך נשמת אפכם ונקבוביות עורכם; נוזליכם העכורים – דרך פיכם
ועורכט, ונך מבעד לנקבובית וחלוליכם. הדברים האלה הלוא תראו בעיניכם
וריחו בנחיריכם ותמשטו בידיכם. והיה בהשתחרר גופכם מכל חטאיכם
וטומאתכם – יטהר דמכם ויהי כדמה של אמא-אדמה וכקצף הנחל המפזז לאור-
השמש; ונשמת-אפכם תטהר וונה – כריח-הניחוח של העולה העולה הפרחים; ובטרבכם
כבשר הברי המבצבץ צח ואדום מבין עלוות-הבלילנות, ומאור עיניכם – כה
בהיר וכה צח, כזרוח השמש בתכלט השמים; ומענה ישרתוכם כל מלאכי אמא-
אדמה, ונשמת אפכם דמכם ובשרכם יהיו אוידים עם נשמת אפה,דמה ובשרה של
אמא-אדמה – למען זהא רוחכם אף היא אחידה עם רוחו של אביכם שבשמים. כי
באמונה – לא יסיג שום איש את זהב שבשמים אלא באמצעות אמא-אדמה.

באשר הרך הנולד לא יוכל להבין את דברי חנוכו של אביו, עד אם לא
טפל בו קודם אמו הורתו – תינוקהו, ורחצנו תיפנו ותלפפו. כל עוד הילד
רך יכירנו מקומו אצל אמו יולדתו ועליו למלא אחר מצוותיה. ולכשיגדל
הילד – יקחנו אביו למען יעבוד לצדו בשדה. והוא יטוב אל אמו בבוא שעת
סעודת הצהרים ולעת ארוחת הערב. אזי ילמדנו אביו דעת, וידריכו ויאמן
בעבודה, ועת בוא העת, כאשר אביו נוכח כי אכן, קלט הבן את חרתו,ונטיב
לעשות את מלאכתו, ימסור האב את כל אחזונתיו לנחלה לבנו האהוב, למען
ימשיך בפועל כפיו. באמונה אני אומר לכם – אשרי הבן השומע בקול אמו
והולך בעצתה. ואשרי הבן למען יארכיכון ימיך על פני האדמה הזאת. אפס –
אומר אני לכם: בני-אדם, כבדו את אמכם אדמה וקיימו כל מצוותיה,למען
יארכיכון ימיכם על האדמה הזאת, וכבדו את אביכם שבשמים למען תזכו לחיי-
נצח בשמים.

באשר האב שבשמים גדול מאה מונים מכל אב העושי מזרע ומדם וגדולה
האם השמימית מכל אם מלידה. ויקר הוא בן-האדם בעיני אביו שבשמים
ואמו – אדמה – רב יותר משיקרים ילדים בעיני אביהם העושי מזרע ודם
ובעיני אמם אשר מלידה. ונבונים יותר הם הדברים והמצוות של אביכם
שבשמים ואמכם-אדמה מאשר דבריהם ומצוותיהם של כל האבות העושים
מזרע ודם והאמהות מלידה. כן גדולה לאין ערוך היא מורשתם של אביכם
שבשמים ואמכם-אדמה – מלכות הנצח של חיי העולם הזה וחיי עולם הבא –
מכל מורשת אבותיכם העושיים זרע ואצאתיכם מלידה.

ואחיכם האמתיים הם אלה המקיימים את מצוות אביכם שבשמים ואמכם
האדמה, ולא אחיכם לדם. באמונה אני אומר לכם כי אויכם האמתיים
המפלשיים אחר חוקים של האב שבשמים ואמא-אדמה, ואהובים אלף מונים
יותר מאשר אויכן לדם. כי מאז ימי קין והבל, כאשר אחיו לדם הפרו
חוקה אלוה – פסה אחווה אמיתית שעל-פי דם ואחים פוגעים באחיהם
כבזרים. על כן אני אומר לכם: אהבו את אחיכם האמתיים לקיום מצוות
אלוה אלף מונים יותר מאשר את אויכם לדם.

"כי אביכם שבשמים הוא א א ה ב ה
"כי אמכם-אדמה היא – א א ה ב ה
"כי בן-האדם הוא – ז ה א ה ב ה
כי האהבה היא המאוחדת את האב שבשמים ואת אמא-אדמה ואת בן-האדם
לשלמות אחת. באשר רוח האדם נבראה מרוחו של האב בשמים, וגופו מגופה
של אמא-אדמה. היו איפוא שלמים כאשר שלמה רווח של האב בשמים וגויה
של אמא-אדמה. אכן, אהבו את אביכם שבשמים כאשר הוא אוהב את רוחכם
אכן, אהבו את אמכם-אדמה כאשר היא אוהבת את גופכם; אכן, אהבו את
אחיכם האמתיים כאשר אוהבים אותם אביכם שבשמים ואמכם-אדמה. אזי
יאציל לכם אביכם שבשמים מרוח הקודש, ואמכם-אדמה ועניק לכם מגופה
הקדוש, ובני האדם כאחים אמתיים, יהגו אהבה איש לרעהו, היא האהבה
אשר קבלוה מידי אביהם שבשמים ואמא-אדמה. והיו כלם עושים אך טוב
האחד למשנהו. ונסר אזי און ואנחה מעל פני האדמה והשמחה
תהא מנת חלקכם. ואז תהא האדמה כשמים ומלכות ה' תופיע. אז יבוא
בן-האדם בכל הדרו לרשת מלכות שדי, ובני האדם יתחלקו אז ביניהם
במורשתנו הקדושה, במלכות שדי. באשר בני האדם יחיו באביהם שבשמים
ואמם-אדמה, ואביהם שבשמים ואמם-אדמה יחיו בהם, ואז – עם מלכות שדי
יבוא קץ הימים. כי אהבת האב שבשמים מעניקה לכל חיי עולם במלכות-
השמים. כי האהבה היא נצחית ועזה האהבה מן המות.

"ועתה הנני מדבר אליכם בלשונו הוויה של אל חי, וברוחו הקדושה של
אבינו שבשמים. עדין אין בכם איש אחד אשר יוכל לתפוס שמץ מכל הדברים
האלה שאני מגיד. זה המבולל לפניכם את התורה מדבר אליכם בלשון מתה,
משל אנשים מתים ובמצעות גופו ידוע-יהלי ובן-התמותה. אותו יכולים
איפוא להבין כל הנשים; באשר כל הנשים הם ידנועי-חלי ובני תמותה.
אין בהם איש הרואה את אור החיים. איש סומא נוהג באחיו הטומא נופלים
העופלים של הטומא המחלה והסבל, עד שבסופו של דבר כלם יחדיו נופלים
אלי בור שחת.
"אני שלוח אליכם מאת האב למען האיר לפניכם את אור-החיים. האור
מאיר לעצמו וגם לחשכה ואילו החושך יודע רק את עצמו ואינו יודע את
האורה. רבים הדברים אשר יש בידי לאמור לכם, אך עדין אינכם מסוגלים
לשאתם. באשר עיניכם רגילים לחשכה ואורו המלא של האב בטשיט עלול
לסנוורכם. כי על כן טרם תוכלו להבין את הדברים אשר אני אומר לכם
בדבר האב שבשמים אשר שלחני אליכם. לכן, איפוא, מחילה לפי חוקי אמכם
אדמה אשר סרבת לכם אודתם. ורק כאשר אביכה יסהרו ויחדשו את גופכם
ויוזקו את עיניכם – תוכלו לשאת באורו של אביגו שבשמים. כי כאשר
תוכלו להסתכל באורה החזק של השמט בצהרים מבלי למצמץ בעינים – אז
יהיה בידכם לשאת גם באורו המסנוור של אביכם בשמים, אשר הוא אלף מונים
מזק יותר מאלף שמשות. אפס כיצד תוכלו לחזות באור המסנוור של אביכם
שבשמים כשאין אתם יכולים למאת אפילו באורה של שמש הזורחת? האמנו
לי: השמש הנה אך כשלהבת הנר בצד סמס-האמת של האב שבשמים. על כן
האמינו איפוא, וקוו ואהבו. באמונה אני אומר לכם: לא יחסכו מכם שלומי-
כם. אם תאמינו בדברי – תהיו מאמינים בשולחי, שהוא אדון-הכל והכל-
יכול. כי כל מה שנמנע מכחם של בני-אדם יכול להעשות ביד האלהים. אם
תאמינו במלאכי אמא-אדמה וחלכו בחקותיה, אמונתכם תצעדכם, ולא תיראו

כל מחלה. שאפו איפוא, ,תקוה גם מאהבתו של אביכם שבשמים ; כי כל
הבוטח בו לא ייכזב לעולם אף לעד לא יראה מות. אהבו איש את אחיו
כי אלהים הוא אהבה ,וכך ידעו מלאכיו כי הולכים אתם בעקבותיו. אז
יתיצבו לפניכם כל המלאכים וישרתוכם, והשטן וכל החטאים והחלאים
והטומאה, יזנחו את גופכם לעד. לכו כפרו על עונותיכם וסלקום.
הטהרו למען תתחדשו ,ולא תוסיפון לחטוא עוד.

וישוע קם, אך כל העם דבקו במקומם, באשר כל אחד מהם חש בעצמת
דברו, ואז הופיע הירח המלא מבין מפלשי העבים ויפן את ישוע בזיוו
וניצוצם נתזו משער ראשו ויעמוד בתוכם לאור הירח ,והוא כמרחף באויר.
איש לא נע ולא זע מבלי נשמע קולם,ולא ידע איש כמה זמן חלף, כי
נדם הזמן.

אז פשט להם ישוע ידיו ויאמר: "יהי השלום עמכם" ויעלם כהעלם משב
הרוח בלטפו את עלי האילנות.

ותוסף העדה לשבת דום על מקומה עד בוש; ורק לאחר מכן נעורו אחד
אחד בדמה כמתוך חלום ממושך, אך איש מהם לא אבה ללכת כשדבריו של
זה אשר עזבם עדין מהדהדים בתוך אזניהם, וימשיכו לשבת כאילו האזינו
לקול מנגינה נפלאה. אך לבסוף אחד - כמתוך חרדת-לילה זה לעד" ועוד
הדבר להיות כאן". ויאמר האחר: "מי יתן ונמשך לילה זה לעד" ועוד
אחרים: "מי יתן והיה הוא עמנו תמיד" - "באמת ובאמונה שליחו של
האלהים הוא כי נטע בנו את התקוה בלבבנו". ולא אבה איש ללכת לביתו באמרם:
"לא אלך הביתה,מקום שם הכל אפל ונעדר חדוה. שלמה נלך לביתנו ואין
שם איש אשר יאהבנו?" והם דברו כן, באשר היו כלם כמעט,עניים, פחחים,
עורים, נכים,קבצנים וגנולי בית;ויהיו הם מאוסים בגנולותם,ורק מרחמים
נסבלו בבתיה מקום שם מצאו מקלט למשך ימים ספורים בלבד. ואף הללו
אשר לבטח היה להם בית וגם משפחה אמרו: "גם אנו נשאר עמכם" באשר
כל איש הרגיש בלבבו, כי דבריו של זה אשר הלך מהם קשרו את העדה הקטנה
בחוטים נעלמים. ויחושו כולם כי אכן נולדו מחדש. הם ראו לנגד עיניהם
עולם מזהיר, גם כאשר נחבא היה יחד בין הענינים, ובלבות כלם נצנצו ציצי-
הוד מופלאים - פרחי החדוה.

ובזרוח קרני השמש הראשונות על פני האדמה, חשו הכל כי היתה זו
שמשה של מלכות האלהים הממשמשת ובאה, ויצאו בפנים צוהלות להקביל את
פני מלאכי האלהים.

ואנשים רבים חולים וטמאים מלאו אחרי דברי ישוע ויפנו אל שפת
הנחלים הרודטים מים. ויתפשטו את בגדיהם ונעליהם,,ויצומו ויפקירו
גופם בידי מלאכי האויר, המים ואור השמש. ומלאכי אמא-אדמה אמרו
אליהם ויחדרו לכל אברי גופם,מבית ומחוץ, וכולם ראו בצאת החטאים
הפגולים והטומאה עד מהרה מתוך גופם.

ורוח אפם של אחדים מהם העלתה צחנה כה גדולה כאשר תסריח הצואה
ואחרים הפריטו כיח רב ורדיחות רעים וקיא-צואה מתוך גופם. כל החלאה
הזאת חלחלה דרך פיהם מין זיעה נתעבת ודוחה מבעד עיניהם ואזניהם. והיו
כאלה אשר כל גופם העלה מין זיעה נתעבת ודוחה מבעד לנקבוביות עורם
ועל אברים שונים פרחו מורסות, אשר בהבקען עד מהרה נתבקעו ותפרסנה
מגולה מצחינה ושתן רב קלח מגופם. והיו מהם אשר השתן שהטילו היה
סמיך כמראה הדבש, ,ושל אחרים מראהו היה כמעט אדום או שחור, או אף
מנובש כחול הנהר. והיו רבים אשר שהתקן מתוכם הבל סרוח כרדן-אפם
של שעירים, ותעל מהם צחנה כבדה עד לבלי נשוא. ויהי בהטהרם -
ויחדר לתוכם מלאכי המים, וכהגיח אשר ממעלה ההרים כן פרצו מתוך גופם
של חטאיהם הנוסנים, וכהגיח אשר ממעלה ההרים כן פרצו מתוך גופם
הפגולים - קשים וגולולים. ויזדקקו בגי הקרקע פאד, ותרב הבאשה
עד כי לא עצר איש לעמוד בה. והסתיו עזבו את הקרקע בדמות רימה
ותולעלה למכביר, אשר בחשו בלשלטתם עד לזעוה ויתפתלו בזעם אין-אונים
לאחר שלמלאך המים מתוך הדיחם מעירם של בני האדם. ואז יחל בהם מלאך
השמש את קרניו ויך עד כי כלו בעוית יסוריהם וי'יסו תחת עצמת קרניו.
וכל האנשים היו רועדים מפחד ברואתם לעיניהם או,,ל תועובות השטן אשר
הושיעום המלאכים מידיהם. ויתנו תודה לאלוהם אשר שלח להם את מלאכיו
למען יגאלו, וישרדו בינותהם אחדים אשר ענו ביסוריהם כבדים אשר לא
הרפו מהם, ולא ידעו מה עליהם לעשות - ויגמרו אומר לשלוח איש אחד
אל ישוע, כי עז היה רצונם כי יהיה הוא עמהם.

ויהי כאשר יצאו שנים לבקשו – ויירא לפניהם ישוע עצמו כשהוא
עולה לקראתם עם הנחל. וימלא לבם תקוה וגיל בשמעם את ברכתו: "השלום
לכם". ותרבינה השאלות אשר היו עם לבם לשאלו – אך מרוב תדהמתם לא
ידעו כיצד יפתחו; כי נסתרו מהם. ויאמר להם ישוע: "הנני בא – באשר
אתם נזקקים לי". ויקרא אחד מהם: "אדוננו – אמנם נזקקים אנו לך –
בוא נא והושיענו מן הענויים!"

וידבר אליהם ישוע בלשון משלים: "נדמיתם לבן החוטא אשר במשך שנים
רבות זלל וסבא, וכל ימיו עברו עליו בהוללות והפקרות בין חבר מרעיו
ובכל שבוע ללא ידיעת אביו – עשה חובות חדשים ואף פזד כסף תרופות
תוך ימים ספורים. והמלוים היו תמיד סוקלים לו מטון באשר לאביו היה
עשר רב וינהג לפרע בסבלנות את חובות בנו. אך לשוא היה מרעיף בנעם
דברי מוסר באזני בנו – כי לא אבה הבן שמוע לתוכחת אביו אשר אף התחנן
לפניו כי לא יוסיף לשרך דרכיו בלי קץ וגבול ,ונוטב כי יצא לשדות
להשגיח על עבודת משרתיו. והנה היה מבטיחהו כל דבר בתנאו כי יפרע
עבורו את החובות הנושנות, אך למחרת היה חוזר לסורו. וכך במשך יותר
משבע שנים, המשיך הבן בחייו המופקרים,עד שפקעה לבסוף,סבלנותו של
האב ולא שלם עוד למלוים ברבית את חובות בנו. "אם אמשיך לפרוע תמיד
את החובות – לא יהי קץ לעוונותיו של בני" ואז המלוים – בזעמם כי
רב – לקחו את בן העשיר להיות להם לעבד , ויעבידוהו יום יום בפרך כדי
שיפרע להם בכך את הממון אשר לוה. ויבוא הקץ על הזלילה והסביאה
וההוללות כל הימים. מבקר עד ערב השקה בזעת אפיו את השדות וכל
אבריו כאבו עליו מרב העמל אשר לא הסכין לו. ויחי על לחם צר ויבש
באין סבר סבר מה להדסיבו בלתי אם בדמעותיו. וכעבור שלשה ימים, לאמר
שהבן סבל סבל מרוב יגיעה ומחום השרב, פנה אל בעליו ויאמר: אין
בכחי לעבדך יותר כי כל אברי כואבים עלי לבלתי נשוא. עד מתי תענה אותי
בפרך? – 'עד אשר ימלאו הימים ויגיע כפוך יכסה על כל חובותיך, ורק
כתם שבע שנים תצא לחפשי' וימרד הבן האומלל בבכי ויאמר: לא אוכל
שאת יותר ולו רק במשך שבע ימים; אנא אנהג כי אם צוורב באגרי הדואבים'
אך הנושה הערץ קרא אליו בחמתו: 'חטמך בעבודתך חיש מהר. אתה אשר
יכולת להוציא ימיך ולילותיך בהוללות שבע שנים תמימות, חייב הנך לעבוד
עתה משך שבע שנים. – לא אמחל לך דבר עד אם תפרע לי את כל חובותיך עד
לפרוטה האחרונה. והבן עם אביו הרצועים חזר מיואש,לעבודתו בשדה.
ויעצור בקרוב כח לעמוד הכן על רגליו מחמת עיפפורו ויסורין – עד אשר
הגיע היום השביעי – הוא יום השבת, אשר בן אין איש עובד בשדה. אז
אסף הבן שארית כחותיו וישרך דרכו אל בית אביו, ויפל ארצה לרגליו
ויאמר: 'אבא, האמינה לי לו רק בפעם הזאת ומחל נא על כל העלבונות
אשר גרמתי לך. נשבע אני כי לא אוסיף לחיות עוד חיי הוללות,ואמלא
אחר כל מצוותיך. אנא, פדני נא מידי זה האיש המדכאני. הבט בי אבי
וראה את אבריו הרצועים ואל נא תכבד עוד את לבך' – ויקרו דמעות-נחם
בעיני האב ויאסוף את הבן אל בין זרעותיו ויאמר: 'הבה נגילה איפפא
ונשמח, כי היום הזה מצאתי מחדש את בני שאבד לי. וילבישנו מחלצות
וישמח וייעלזו כל היום. ויהי למחרת, ויתן לבנו שקל כסף על
מנת שישלם לנושיו את כל חובותיו, ושוב נא הגיד לך לאמור: 'רואה
אתה בני, כי הנקל לפשות חובות גדולים במשך שבע שנים של חיי הוללות
אך מה קשה לפרוע בעבודה קשה במשך שבע שנים'. – 'אבי, אמת נכון הדבר
כי קשה,מה קשה לפרעם, ואפילו נתן לעשות כן בשגני שנים בלבד'! ויוסף
האב להסיף לו לאמור: 'אכן רק בפעם הזאת הורשה לך להשלים את חובותיך
תוך שבעת ימים תחת שבע שנים, וכל השאר מחול לך. אך שים נא אל לב
בני, כי לא תוסיף יותר לעשות חובות לעולם. כי באמת אני אומר לך –
שום איש בלעדי אביך לא ימחל יכול לך את החובות, באשר אתה בנו. כי אצל כל
איש מלבדו היה עליך לעבל לעבול קשה במשך שבע שנים תמימות ככתוב בחוקותינו'.

'אבי, מעתה אהיה לך בן אוהב ומסור ולא אוסיף יותר לעשות חובות
כי עתה ידעתי מה קשה לפרעם'. ויצא אל שדות אביו ויפקח יום-יום על
עבודת פועליו, אך מעולם לא העביד את פועליו קשות כי זכר את עבודתו
הוא,הקשה. ויהי מקץ שנים ותגדלה ותפרוצנה נחלות אביו תחת ידו כי
היתה ברכת האב שרויה במעשי-ידיו. ומעט-מעט הוא החזיר לאביו עשרת
מונים מכל אשר בזבז במשך שבע שנים. והיה כאשר ראה האב כי הטיב
הבן לנצל את עבודת פועליו ואת הכנסות אחוזותיין – ויאמר לו:'בני
רואה אני כי נכסי נתונים בידים נאמנות. הנני מוסר לך את כל המקנה
את ביתי, את קרקעותי ואוצרותי. יהיו איפפוא,כל אלה לך למורשת. הוסף
והגדילם למען יגל לבי בך, וכאשר יקבל הבן יירדר את ירושת אביו
וימחל את החובות לכל החיים אשר ידם לא השיגה לשלם. ויברכם אלהים
בחיים ארוכים,ברוב בנים ובעשר רב, על כי היה טוב לעבדיו ורחום
למקנהו".

113

אז פנה ישוע אל האנשים החולים ויאמר: "מדבר אני אליכם במשלים
למען תיטיבו להבין דבר ה'. שבע שנות הזילה 'והביאה וחיי ההוללות
הללא המה חטאי העבר. הנושה האכזר – הלוא הוא השטן. החובות המה
המחלות. העבודה הקשה – המה הכאבים. הבן הפזרן – הנכם אתם. פרעון
החובות הלוא היא התנערותכם מן השדים והחלים, ולרפואת גופכם. כיס הכסף
שניתן מידי האב הוא כוח המשחרר של המלאכים. האב – הריהו האל. נחלתו
של האל הריהם – הארץ והשמים. משרתיו של האב הלוא המה המלאכים. שדהו
של האב היא תבל, אשר ממלכות שדי כשבני האדם יבואו בברית עם מלאכי
עליון לפעול יחדיו. כי אני אומר לכם: הלוא טוב שיישמע הבן למצוות
אביו ויפקח על עבדי אביו בשדה מהיותו חייב לנושה האכזר ומעבדו אותו
בזעת אפו בפרך כדי לפרוע את כל חובותיו. כן מוטב שבני האדם ימלאו
אחר מצוותיו של האב שבשמים וישן שכמם יחד עם מלאכי האב במלכותו מאשר
ייעשו לבעלי חובו של השטן – אדוני השאול, החטאים וכל החלאים הרעים,
ונמקו ביסוריהם תוך עבודה קשה ויזע, עד אשר יפרעו כל חובותיהם.

באמנה אני אומר לכם: רבים ועצומים חטאיכם. שנים על שנים נמשכתם
אחר מדוחי השטן. והייתם זוללים וסובאים ושוטפי זמה, וחובותיכם גדלו מאז
כפליים. הנה הגיעה השעה שעתכם לפרוע ויקשה מכם הפרעון ויכבד. אל נא תאבדו
איפוא סבלנותכם עוד לאחד היום השלישי, כאשר קרה לבן הפזרן – אלא אחכו
באורך רוח עד היום השביעי אשר קודש ביד האלהים. אז תלכו בלב סך ונכנע
לבמצב לפני צביכם שבשמים למען יסלח לכם עוונותיכם וימחל כל חובותיכם
הנושנים. באמונה אני אומר לכם: אהב את יאהבכם אביכם שבשמים שבעה ימים. אלה אשר
מצרים. בהתרדו לכם פליון בצום ותפילה – אז – לעומת כל יום נוסף בו
נתחייבו בבריאותם על חטאיהם במשך שבע שנים, אולם מלשלמים תמורתם באמונה
ובקפידה עד ליום השביעי – להם אביכם שבשמים ימחל את חובות כל שבע
השנים".

"ואם ירבו חטאינו שבע שנים כפול שבע?" שאל אחד חולה אשר סבלו כבד
מנשוא.

"גם במקרה זה ימחל לכם האב שבשמים את כל חובותיכם במשך שבעה ימים
כפול שבע".

"אשרי המתמידים עד הקץ, באשר שליחי השטן כותבים את כל מעשיכם הרעים
עלי ספר. הוא ספר גופכם ורוחכם. באמונה אומר אני לכם: – אין אף מעשה
רע אשר לא נרשם מאז היות העולם מלפני אביו שבשמים. כי יש בידכם להמלט
מידי החוקים שעשו בידי מלכים, אך מחוקיו של אל עליון לא ימלט בשר ודם.
וביום בואכם לפני האלהים יעידו שליחי השטן על מעשיכם, והאלהים יראה את
חטאיכם כתובים בספר גופכם ורוחכם, ויעגם אל לבו. אך אם תנחמו על מעשיכם
ותכפרו פני מלאכי עליון בצום ותפילה – אזי – לעומת כל יום נוסף בו
תצומו ותתפללו – ימחו המלאכים שנה נוספת ממעשיכם הרעים מתוך ספר גופכם
ורוחכם. והיה כאשר תמחק ותסתר מן הדף האחרון שארית חטאיכם, תיכבו
הכן לפני האלהים וישמח אלהים אל ביתו ויצוה על כל מסרתי ומלאכי
השטן ומן הסלות. הוא יאספכם אל תוך תראו עוד מחלה ורעע, והיה אז
מאז ואילך – תחת לחטוא, תבלו ימיכם בעשיית מעשים טובים. באמת אני אומר לכם: ירושתו מלאכי
האלהים את מעשיכם בספר גופכם ורוחכם. באמת אני אומר לכם: לא נעשה
כל מעשה טוב אשר לא נרשם 'מלפני ה'' מאז היות העולם, באשר יכולים אתם
לצפות לשוא לחסדיהם של מלכיכם ומושליכם, אך לעולם לא ייחסך שכרכם עבור
מעשיכם הטובים מיד האל.

"ורבעת עמדכם אל מול פני האלהים – יעידו מלאכיו עליכם לפי מעשיכם
הטובים. והאלהים יראה את מעשיכם הטובים והנם כתובים בגופכם וברוחכם,
וישמח אל לבו. ויברך אלהיכם את גופכם ואת רוחכם וכל מעשיכם, ויתן לכם
למורשה את מלכותו שבשמים ובארץ תחיו בה עד עולם. אשרי האיש
היכול לבוא במלכות שדי, כי לא יירא מות עד לעולם."

ותדם דממה כבדה בתום דבריו, והללו אשר היו נואשים לבשו תקוה ועוז
מאמרי פיו וימשיכו לצום ויתפללו. ואותו איש אשר דבר אליו לראשונה
פתח ואמר: "אנכי אתאמץ להתמיד עד היום השביעי", והשני אף הוא אמר:
"גם אני אשתדל להתמיד עד תום שבעת הימים כפול שבע".

ויען להם ישוע: "אשרי אלה אשר ידעו להתמיד עד הסוף, כי יזכו לרשת את האדמה".

ויהיו ביניהם חולים רבים אשר עונו במכאובים קשים, והמה זחלו בכבדות עד למרגלות ישוע, כי לא יכלו יותר להלך על רגליהם ויאמרו: "אדונינו, מעונים אנו ביסורים גדולים. אמור נא לנו מה נעשה?" ויראו לישוע את רגליהם אשר בלטו בהן עצמות נכוות ומעוקמות, ויאמרו: "לא מלאך חאניר ולא סלאף חמים ואף לא זה של אור השמש הקלו על מכאובינו - וזאת על אף צומנו ותפלותנו וסבילותנו, ואנו מלאנו אחר כל דבריך כלם".

"אמנם אני אומר לכם: עצמותיכם יעלו ארוכה. אל נא תאמרו בואאו. לכן בקשו את עזרתו של רופאה-העצמות הלוא הוא מלאך האדמה, כי הימנה לוקחו עצמותיכם ואליה ישובון." ויושט ידו לעבר שפת חנחל אשר שם רסכו חמים חמדדים וחום השמש את העפר ויהפכוהו לחמר בצקי.

"חשקיעו רגליכם במדמנה למען יוציא מלאך-האדמה בחבוקו את כל חסן מאה ומלאאה מתוך עצמותיכם. ואתם תראו בעיניכם את השטן ואת מכאוביכם בחמלטם בעוד האדמה חובקת את אבריכם הכאובים, ובליסות עצמותיכם תעלמנה תאיפרנה ובא הקץ ליסוריכם." וימלאו החולים אחר דבריו בידעם כי אמנם ירפאו.

ויהיו אחדים מן החולים אשר המשיכו לסבול קשות ממכאוביהם על אף הקפידם בצומם. כוחם אזל וגום ורחום הקדחת ענה את גופם, ובגרצותם לקום ממסותיהם לגשת אל ישוע - סבב עליהם ראשם יאטם כבררוח תזזית. ויהי בנסותם לקום ולהלך כן כרעו שכבו חמרי אונים.

ויקרב אליהם ישוע ויאמר: "אתם סובלים באשר השטן וחלאיו מענים את גופכם. אך אל לכם לחשוש, כי עד מהרה יבוא הקץ לשליטתם עליכם. כי דומה השטן לאיש חיפה הנכבד, לברת סכנו בעת העדרו מן הבית בכוונה לקחת את רכושו ולהעבירו לביתו הוא. וילט מישהו את אזנו של בעל הבית כי משתולל אויבו בתוך חצריו. וירץ וישר אל הבית, והשכן הרע, אשר הספיק כבר לאסוף כל דבר ערך אשר חמד בו - הבחין בבעל-הבית הממהר לחזור מרחוק וימלא עברה וזעם כי בגבר מסנו לקחת הכל וילאל למבר ולהסחים בחפציו ולעשות בהם כלה, כן שאם לו לא יהיו - לפחות אל יאשאר מהם שריד גם לבעלם. אך בעל-הבית נכנס מיד ובטרם היה ספק בידי השכן הרע להפיק את זמם תפסו וישליכו מחוץ לבית. באמת אני אומר לכם: בדומה לכך חדר השטן אל גופכם שחוא משכנו של האלהים. וישתלט על כל דבר אשר חפץ לרשתו: את נשמת אפכם דמכם, עצמותיכם, בשרכם, מעיכם, עיניכם ואזניכם, אך בצומכם ובתפילתכם חחזרתם אליכם את אדוני גופכם ואת מלאכיו. ועתה בראות השטן כי חוזר אדוננו האמתי של גופכם וכי בא הקץ לשלטונו, ולאסוף בחלונו את שארית אונו כדי להסחית בגדפכם ילעשות בו כלה בטרם יספיק הצדון להגיעו. כי על כן מענה אתכם השטן כה נמרצת בחושו כי הנה בא הקץ, אך אל נא יחר לבבכם כי עד מהרה יופיעו מלאכי האלהים לשכון שוב בבית מגוריהם ולהכשירו לשמש כמשכן האלהים מחדש. הם יתפשו את השטן ויטלטלוהו וישליכוהו מתוך גופכם עם כל חלאיו וכל תרעבותיו גם יחד, ומאושרים תהיו אז באשר קבל תקבלו את גמולכם על שאמץ עמידתכם האיתנה ולא תיראון עוד כל מחלה וכל נגע.

ויהי ביניהם אחד אשר סבל מעניויי השטן יותר מכל האחרים, וכל גופו צפד ויהי כשלד, ועור ויהי בשרו הצהיב כעלה אשר בסלכת, וכה חלם היה עד כי לא יכל לזחול ולחלך זי יבכש אוורלי על ידיו, ורק זעק זעק אליו מרחוק: "רחם נא אדון, כי מאז קם העולם ויהי - לא ראה אדם סבל כי אם כה נורא כמוני. יודע אני כי שולחת מאת חי באמת, ואני יודע כי אם יש אם רצונך, תוכל לגלש מקרבי את השטן כהרף עין. האין מלאכי האלהים נשמעים לשליחו של אלהים? בואה אדון וסלק עתה מתה מגופי את השטן כי משתולל הוא בקרבו בחימה שפוכה ואיום ונורא הוא-העינויים".

ויען ישוע: "השטן יענה אותך קשו. באשר כבר צמת ימים רבים, ואין אתה משלם לו את המס. אינך מזין אותו עוד בכל התועבות אשר בהן שיחת עד כה את מקדש רוחך. הנך מענה את השטן ברעב, ובעבור זה יענה גם הוא אותך. אל תירא כי אני אומר לך: השטן יישמד בטרם יהרס גופך אתה. כי כאשר תך צם ומתפלל מלאכי האלהים מגינים על גופך בפני פגיעות השטן וזמם של השטן חסר אונים הוא לעמות מלאכי אלוה". ויבראו כולם למבל ישוע ויתחננ אליו בקול גדול: "רחם נא עליו, אדון, כי רב-סבלו מכל כלון, ואם לא תלפק מקרבו את השטן מיד, יראים אנו כי עד מחר לא ייותר שושוד".

ויען ישוע לאמר: "גדולה היא אמונתכם; לו יהי כפי אמונתכם! ראה תראו עד מהרה פנים אל פנים את פניו הגוראים של השטן ואת יכלתו של בן

האדם . כי הנה אני מגרש מהתוככם את השטן העצום בכח שֶ‏מֵ‏ןֿ התמים , הוא
החלש ביצורי האדון . באשר רוחו הקדושה של האל תהפוך את דלי הכוח ביותר
לחזקים אף מאבירי הכוח . ויחלוב ישוע את הרמלות אשר רעתה באחו , ויתן
את החלב על פני החול שלהם בחום הטמט ואמרו : "ראו , הנה כחו של מלאך-
החלב בא בתוך החלב הזה, ועתה יבוא בו גם כחו של מלאך הטמט ." ויחם החלב
בעוצם חומו של הטמט .

"ועתה מלאכי המים והטמט יתאחדו עם מלאך האויר"

והנה אדי החלב החם החלו עולים בלאט ומתמזגים עם האויר .

"בוא ושאף אל קרבך בעד פיך את עצמתם של מלאכי המים הטמט והאויר
כדי שתכנס לתוך גופך ותגרש הטמט מקרבך" . והאיש החולה המעונה מידי
הטמט , שאף עמוקות אל תוכד את האד הלבנבן המתמר ועולה .

"מיד יעזוב הטמט את גופך , כי מאז שלשת ימים הוא גורע את מכפן כי לא
נמצא לו כל מזון בקרבך . יצוא יצא מתוך גופך להשביע את רעבונו אשר הצ‏יק
לו מזה שלשה ימים ." אך בן האדם ישמיד את גופו על מנת שלא יענה עוד
איש לעולם ." ואז נאחז גופו של החולה עוית ויתמתח כמו להקיא - ולא יכול.
ויאבק על נשימתו כי נעצרה לפתע , ויפול מתעלף בחיק ישוע .

"עתה הנה יוצא הטמט מגופו - ראו!" ויש‏טוע הורה בידו לעבר פיו " ‏פעור
של החולה ויראו כולם בתמהון ופחד בצאת הטמט מתוך פיו בדמות תולעת אימה
אל טול אדי החלב. ויקח ישוע שתי אבנים חדות בידיו וימחץ את ראש הטמט
וימשוך מתוך גרונו של החולה את גופה המפלצת אשר ארכה היה כמעט כמידת
ארכו של אדם . והיה בצאת התעלעת המתועבת מתוך גרונו של החולה - ותחש
אליו מיד רוח אפו וכהרף עין חדלו כל הכאבים . ויראו כולם ברגשי פחד
את גופו המבעית של הטמט .

" ראה את החיה המבעיתה אשר נשאת וטפחת בתוך גופך שנים רבות . אני
גרשתיך מתוכך והרגתיו כדי שלא יוסף לענותך עוד לעולם . תן תודה לאלהים
על כי מלאכיו חלצו אותך ממנו , ואל תחטא עוד לבל ישוב הטמט אליך שנית
ויהי נא מעתה גופך למשכן הקודש של האלהים ."

וישתאו כולם לדבריו ‏משעשי גבורתו , ויאמרו: "אדוננו, אכן הנך שליחו
של האלהים וכל סודותיו צלו לפניך".

"ואתם" ענה ישוע "הין נא בניו הנאמנים של אלהים כדי שגם לכם יהיה
חלק בכחו ובמדע סודותיו . כי חכמו ועצמו יתנו לך להשיג רק בכח אהבת האל .
אהבו איפוא את אביכם שבשמים ואת אמכם אדמה בכל לבבכם ובכל מאודכם, ושרתו
אותם למען ישרתו גם אותכם , והיו כל מעשיכם קודש לאלהים . ואל תזונו
את הטמט,כי שכרו של החטא - מות, בעוד שהגמול למעשים הטובים,הנתון ביד
האלהים, הצ‏א האהבה , שהיא הכרתם ועצמתם של חיי עולם." ויכרעו כולם
להודות לה' על ‏אהבתו . וישוע נפרד מהם באמרו: שוב אשוב בשניד לאלה מכם
אשר יעמוד בתפלתם ובצומם עד היום השביעי. יהי השלום עמכם".

והאיש החולה אשר ישוע גרש מקרבו את הטמט, קם ויעמוד על רגליו כי
חזר אליו אונו , וישאף עמוקות ועיניו סהרו , כי חלפו עברו כל מכאוביו .
ויסיל עצמו ארצה,על המקום אשר עליו עמד ישוע, וישק את עקבות רגליו
ויבך .

ויהי ליד עמק ‏עדֵ‏ק-הנחל וחולים רבים צמו ויתפללו עם מלאכי האלהים שבעה
ימים ושבעה לילות . ויהי שכרם גדול כי מלאו,אחר דברי ישוע . ויהי מקץ
שבעת הימים, ויתמו כל יסוריהם, ובעלות השמט באפם ויראו והנה ישוע עולה
לקראתם מן ההר ו‏אמר:השמט ‏ספת‏ים לרא‏שו.

"הַשְלום·לכם"

ולא ענו אותו דבר כי אם נפלו לרגליו ויגעו בטולי בגדו בתודה על
רפואתם .

"תנו תודה לא לי , כי אם לאמא-אדמה אשר שלחה את מלאכיה לרפא לכם.
לכו איפוא , ואל נא תחטאו בשנית למען לא תראו עוד חלי ומדוה והיו המלאכים
לטגן" . אך המה ענו לו: "אנה נלך אדוננו, ומאמרי פיך טרופא בשורת
חיי עולם . הגד נא לנו, מה המה החטאים אשר עלינו להמנע מהם, כדי שלא
נירא עוד כל מחלה?" וישוע ענה: "יהי כן, כפי אמונתכם,"ויטב בינותם
ויאמר:

"הלוא כה נאמר בימי קדם: 'כבד את אביך שבשמים ואת אמא-אדמה למען
יאריכון ימיך על פני האדמה', ובסמוך לכך ניתנה הדברה: 'לא תרצח' באשר

116

החיים נתנו לכל מידי אלוה ואת אשר חלק אלהים, אל לו לאדם לשלול במו ידיו
כי באמונה אני אומר לכם – מאם אחת נתנו חיים לכל אשר באפו רוח, על פני
האדמה הזאת. על כן כל הרוצח, את אחיו הוא רוצח, וממנו תסתיר אמא-אדמה
את פניה ותשלול את דדיה המזינים. ואף מלאכיה יתעלמו ממנו והשטן יקבע
את משכנו בגופו. ובשרה של חיה הרוגה בתוך מעיו תיהפך לו לקברו. כי
באמת אני אומר לכם: כל הרוצח – את עצמו הוא רוצח, וכל הנזון מבשרן של
חיות מומתות, מבשר-גופו של מר המות הוא ניזון. כי כל ספה מדם הפגרים
הופכת ארס בתוך דמו, ורוח פיהם לסחון בפיו, ובשרם יהיה לכיבים בבשרו
ועצמותיהם – לגיר בעצמיו, ומעיהם – לרקב במעיו, ועיניהם יהיו לתבלולים
בעיניו, ואזניהם יביאו זיבת שעוה מתוך אזניו, ומרתם יסב למותו הוא.
כי רק בשרתכם את האב שבשמים ומחלים כם החוננים את שבע השנים בשבעה
ימים. אך השטן אינו מוחל לכם דבר ועליכם לפרוע לו עבור הכל: עין תחת
עין, שן תחת שן, יד תחת יד, רגל תחת רגל, כויה תחת כויה, פצע תחת פצע,
חיים תחת חיים, מות תחת מות. כי הגמול על עוון הוא מות. לא תרצחו אף
גם לא תאכלו את בשר סרפכם התמים למען שלא תהיו לעבדיו של השטן. כי על
כן דרך יסורים הוא אל זו המוליכה אלי אבדון. עשו רצונו של ה' למען אשר
ישרתוכם מלאכיו בדרך החיים. מלאו איפוא, אחר מצוותיו: 'הנה נתתי
לכם את כל עשב זורע זרע אשר על פני הארץ, ואת כל העץ אשר בו פרי עץ
זורע זרע לכם יהיה לאכלה. ולכל חית הארץ ולכל עוף השמים ולכל רומש
על הארץ אשר בו נפש חיה, הנני נותן כל ירק עשב לאכלה. וכן את החלב
מכל יצור אשר יש בו רוח חיים יהיה לכם לאכלה. כי כשם שנתתי את פרח
ירק עשב לאכלה כן הנני נותן לכם את חלבם. אפס את הבשר ואת הדם המזין
אותו לא תאכלו. ואדרש את הדם השפוך – זה דמכם אשר הוא גם נפשכם; דרוש
אדרוש את כל חי שנרצח ואת כל נפש אדם שנרצח, כי אני ה' אלהים, אל קנא
ונוקם, פוקד עוון אבות על בנים על שלשים ועל רבעים לשונאי. וסולח
לאלפים סאוהבי ושומרי מצוותיו. ואהבתם את ה' אלהיכם בכל לבבכם ובכל
נפשכם ובכל מאדכם." זוהי הדברה הראשונה והגדולה שבכלן. והשניה –
אף היא חשובה כמוה: 'ואהבת לרעך כמוך' – אין. דברות גדולות מאלו.

ואחר הדברים האלה היו כולם מחשים, פרט לאחד אשר קרא: מה עלי לעשות
אדון, בראותי חיה הטורפת את אחי ביער? האניח לאחי לגווע או מוטב כי
אמית את חית הפרא? אך האם לא אעבור בכך עברה?"

ויען ישוע לאמור: " הלוא כה נאמר להם בימי קדם: כל החיה הרומשת
על הארץ וכל הדגה אשר בים וכל עוף הסלים – אתם תרדו בם. באמונה אני
אומר לכם, כי מכל החי אשר על פני הארץ ברא אלהים את האדם בצלמו.
על כן נבראו החיות למען האנסים ולא אנשים למען חית, ואי אמם עוברים על
החוק בהמיתכם את חית-הפרא כדי להציל את חיי אחיכם, כי אכן, אומר אני
לכם: רב ערכו של האדם מן החיה. אך זה אשר הורג חיה ללא סיבה כשאין
חיה תוקפתו, אלא רק בגלל שאיפה להמיתה או ליהנות מבשרה, או מפרותה,
או לו רק מן השבחון שבפיו – רע הדבר אשר יבוא, כי בכך הופך הוא
להיות חית-טרף בעצמו. ועל כן יהי סופו הוא כסופן של חיות הפרא."

ויאמר האחר: "משה, גדול ישראל, התיר לאבותינו לאכול את בשר הבהמות
הטהורות, ואסר רק את בשרן של הטמאות, ולמה זה הנך אוסר עלינו אכילת
בשרן של כל החיות? איזהו החוק שניתן מאת ה' – האם של משה או שלך?"

ויען ישוע: "ה' נתן לאבותיכם על יד משה עשר דברות, דברות אלו –
חמורות הן – אסרו אבותיכם, ובראותו משה כן – נכסרו רחמיו
על בני עדנו כי לא חפץ באבדנם. ויתן להם עשר דברות כפולות עשר, והן
קלות יותר, למען יוכלו לקיימן. באמונה אני אומר לכם: לו לא היו יכולים
אבותיכם למלא עשרת הדברות של ה' – לא היה ממשה כל צורך בעשרת-
הדברות כפולות עשר. כי זה אשר רגליו עומדות איתן כהר-ציון – אינו
נזקק לקבים. ורק זה אשר אבריו רועדים, הנקל לו להתקדם באמצעות קבים
מאשר בלעדיהן. וכה אמר משה לאלהים: צר לי עמי כי יאבדו באשר
נבערים המה מדעת ואינם מוכשרים להבין את דברותיך. נדמה המה כילדים
אשר עדין מתקשים לתפוס את דברי אביהם. תנה לי אלהי, ואצו לפניהם
חוקים אחרים – למען אשר לא יאבדו. אם לא יהיו עמך – אלהים – הרי
מוטב שלא יהיו נגדך, וכך יוכלו להתקיים עד אשר יבוא היום יום התבגרם
דיים, אזי תגלה להם את מצוותיך. על כן שבר משה את שני לוחות האבן,
עליהם היו חקוקות עשרת הדברות, ויתן להם עשר דברות כפולות עשר תמורתן.
ומעשרת הדברות כפולות עשר אלו, עשו הסופרים והפרושים פי מאה, ויטילו
על שכמכם עול כבד מנשוא, אשר הם עצמם לא ישאונו. כי ככל שהדברות
קרובות יותר לאלהים – אנו נזקקים למיעוטן, וככל שתרחקנה ממנו, צריכים
אנו ליותר מהן. כי על כן רבות המצוות של הסופרים והפרושים מני ספור.
מצוות בן-האדם מנינן שבע; של המלאכים – שלש; ואילו של האלהים – אחת.

"אני מלמדכם איפוא, רק את אותן המצוות אשר אתם עשויים להבינן
כדי שתהיו לאנשים ותוכלו למלא את שבע המצוות של בן-האדם. לאחר מכן
יגלו לכם גם המלאכים את מצוותיהם שלהם על מנת שבסופו של דבר תבוא
בכם רוח קדשו של ה' ותנחה אתכם במצוותיו".

ויהיו כלם משתאים לחכמתו ויבקשוהו לאמר: "המשך אדוננו, ולמדנו
נא את כל המצוות שאנו עשויים לקבלן".

וישוע הוסיף: " אלהים צווה לאבותיכם: "לא תרצח", אך לבם היה
קשה וירצחו, ואז חפץ משה כי לפחות לא ימיתו בני אדם, ויתיר להם
לקטול חיות, אך אז נתקשה לבם של אבותיכם עוד יותר ויקטלו אנשים
וחיות כאחד. אפס אני אומר לכם: אל תקטלו אנשים ולא חיות וכן שום
מזון הבא אל פיכם. כי באם הנכם אוכלים מזון חי, הוא יקיימכם, אך
בקטלכם את מזונכם, המזון המת ימיתכם אף הוא, באשר החיים באים רק
מן החי, בעוד סמן הסטן יבוא רק מות, כי כל דבר הממית את מזונכם
ממית גם את גופיכם, וכל אשר ממית את גופיכם מכלה גם את נשמותיכם.
גופיכם הופכים להיות מה שהנכם מזוניכם, כמו כן רוחכם הופכת להיות
התאם למחשבתכם. על כן לא תאכלו כל דבר אשר אש או קרה או מים
קלקלוהו. כי מזונות שרופים, קפואים או רקובים ישרפו יקפיאו וירקיבו
גם את גופיכם. אל תדמו לחקלאי הסכל אשר זרע זרעים באדמתו זרעים מבושלים
קפואים ורקובים, ויבא הסתיו ובשדותיו את כל דבר, וירב צערו,
והיידם כאותו חקלאי אשר זרע את שדותיו בזרעים חיים, והם נשאו שבלי
חסה מאה שערים מן הזרעים שזרע. כי באמונה אני אומר לכם: חיו לכם
באש של עצמכם אך אל תכינו את מזונכם באשו של המות המכלה את מזונכם
את גופכם ואת נשמותיכם גם יחד".

"אדוננו, איה היא אש חיינו?" שאלו אחדים מהם.
"היא אצורה בכם, בדמכם ובגופכם"
"ואשו של המות?" שאלו אחרים.
"זו היא האש המבוערת מחוץ לגופכם שהיא חמה חמה מדמכם. באש זו של המות
הנכם מבשלים את מזונכם בבתיכם ובשדותיכם. באמת אני אומר לכם: זוהי
האש המכלה את מזונכם ואת גופכם. זוהי אותה האש הזידונית המכלה גם
את מחשבותיכם וגם את חילכם. כי גופכם הוא – מה שהנכם אוכלים,
ורוחכם היא – מה שהנכם חושבים. לא תאכלו איפוא דבר, שאש המות יותר
מאשר אש החיים – המית אותו. על כן הכינו לכם ואכלו מכל פרי עץ
ומכל עשב הצומח בשדה וכל חלב בהמה הטוב למאכל. כי כל אלה ניזונים
ומבשלים באש החיים, וכולם, הם ממתנות אמא-אדמה. אך בל תאכלו כל
דבר אשר אשו של המות נותנת לו את טעמו – כי מן הסטן הוא".

"כיצד נאפה את לחם חוקנו יום-יום ללא אש, אדון?" – שאלו אחדים
מהם בתמהון רב.

"מוטב כי תכינו את לחמכם מלאכי האלהים. השרו את חיטתכם כדי
שמלאך המים יבוא בה, ואז הניחוה באויר על מנת שיציף אותה גם מלאך
האויר, והשארתם אותה מבקר עד ערב לעין השמש, על מנת שמלאך אור-
השמש ירד עליה. אזי תבוא ברכת שלשת המלאכים בחיטתכם ונבטו החיים
יחלו להנץ בה. אזי כתשו את הגרעינים והכינו מהם עוגת מצות כאשר
עשו אבותיכם בצאתם ממצרים, מבית עבדים. ועתה שובו והניחו את המצות
בשמש משעט זריחתה, ובעלות השמש בגבה השמים, הפכום אותן על צדן
כדי, למען יציף גם אותן מלאך אור-השמש, וכך השאירו אותן עד בוא
השמש. באשר מלאכי המים, האויר ואור השמש, הזינו והבשילו את החסה
בשדה, והם הם אשר יכינו גם את לחמכם. ואותו השמש אשר הצמיח והבשיל
את החסה באש של החיים – הוא אשר יאפה באש החיים את לחמכם. כי אש החמה
היא הנותנת חיים לחמה, ללחם ולגוף. אבל אש המות ממיתה את החסה, הלחם
והגוף. והמלאכים החיים של אל חי, משרתים רק אנשים חיים, כי אלהים
הוא אלהי החיים ולא אלהי המתים.

"על כן אכלו תמיד משלחנו של אלהים: את פירות האילנות, את גרעיני
ועשבי השדה, את חלב הבהמות ודבש הדבורים. כי כל דבר מלבד אלה, הוא
השן בעצמך, המוליך בדרך החטאים והמחלות אלי מות. ואילו המזונות
אשר הנכם אוכלים משלחנו המבורך של האלהים, מעניקים כח ועלומים לגופכם
ולא תיראו חלי לעולם. כי שלחנו של אלהים סיפק מחיתו של מתושלח מאז
ומקדם. באמת אני אומר לכם: אם תחיו כאשר חי הוא – יתן גם לכם אלהי
החיים חיים ארוכים על פני האדמה כחייו שלו.

"כי באמונה אני אומר לכם: אלהי החיים עשיר הוא מכל עשירי עולם
ושלחנו הרחב משופע הרבמר"ל שלוחנת ושמחה של גדולי העשירים שבעולם.
אכלו איפוא,כל ימיכם, מעל שלחנה של אמכם-אדמה,ולא תדעון מחסור
ובסעדכם על שלחנה ואכלתם כל דבר ממש כאשר הנך מוצי על שלחן אמא-
אדמה, לא תבשלון ואף לא תערבבון מין בסאינו מינו, למען לא יהפכו
מעיכם צמג מהביל, כי באמת אני אומר לכם: לתועבה היא בעיני ה'.

"כן אל תהיו כאותו עבד שזלל תמיד מעל שלחנו של אדונין את מנות
אחרים והיה מהנה עצמו מכל דבר, וזולל הכל בערבוביה. ובראות אדוניו
כן, ותעל חמתו ויגרשנו מעם השלחן, וכאשר כלו כלם את סעודתם, אסף
ויערבב את כל אשר נותר על השלחן ויקרא אליו את משרתו התאותן,ויאמר
ויאמר: "סול וזלול כל אלה יחד עם החזירים, כי מקומך ביניהם ולא
אצל שלחני".

"השמרו איפוא, לבל תטמאו את היכל גופכם בכל מיני תועבות,
והסתפקתם בשנים או שלשה מיני מזונות בלבד, שאותם תמצאו תמיד על
שלחנה של אמא-אדמה, ואל תתאוו ליהנות מכל דבר שראו סביבכם,
כי באמונה אני אומר לכם: אם תערבבו כל מיני מזונות בתוך גופכם,יבוא
הסוף על שלומכם ומלחמת אין-קץ תסתולל בקרבכם, וכאשר משפחות ואף
ממלכות מפוצגות אבדון על עצמן בשל מסתסה ופירוד, כן תביאו כליה
על גופכם. כי אלהיכם הוא אלהי השלום ולא ישא פירוד. אל תעירו
ואל תעוררו איפוא, את דעם האל,למען לא ירדיפכם מעל שלחנו ולמען
לא תוכרחו לפנות אל שלחנו של השטן אשר אשן,-אם החטאים, המחלה
והמות - תכלה את גופיכם."

"ובאכלכם - אל תאכלו לשבע. נוסו מפתויי השטן והטו אזנכם לקול
מלאכי אלוה. באשר השטן ברוב כחו מפתה אתכם תמיד לאכול עוד ועוד.
ושלטתם ברוחכם ועמדתם בפני מאווי גופכם. צומכם תמיד רצוי בעיני
מלאכי אלהים, על כן שימו אל לבבכם מפעם לפעם מהי כמות המזון שאכלתם
לשובע, בכדי שתתפחיתו מסכה כדי שליש לפעמים הבאות.

"אל יהא משקל מזונכם היומי פחות ממנה, אך ראו לבל תגיע למעלה
מסתי מנה,כי אז ישרתוכם מלאכי אלהים תמיד, ולעולם לא תהיו לעבדי השטן
ותחלואיו. אל תעמיסו על המלאכים עבודת-יתר בריבכם בסעודות מרובות,
כי באמונה אני אומר לכם: האוכל יותר מפעמיים ביום, מקיים בגופו
פעולת השטן, ועד מהרה יסתלק עליו השטן. אכלו איפוא, פעם אחת רק
עם הגיע השמש למרומי השמים, ובשנית, עם שקיעתו. כי אז לא תיראו
חלי, ותשאו חן בעיני ה'. אך אם תאבו להשביע את רצונם של המלאכים
ולהרחיק את השטן כליל מגופיכם - סבו לכם רק פעם אחת ביום ליד שלחנו
של האלהים, למען יאריכון ימיכם על פני האדמה. כי כך ימצא חן בעיני
ה'. אכלו איפוא תמיד כשבשלחנו של ה' ערוך לפניכם ומעד תאכלו מאשר
מצוי על שלחנו של ה' כי באמת אני אומר לכם: יודע האלהים היטב מה
דרוש לגופכם ואימתי הוא דרוש."

"עם בוא החדש אייר אכלו שעורה, ועם בוא סיון אכלו חטה, הטוב
שבכל העשבים המזריעים זרע. ויהי לחם חוקכם יום-יום עשוי חטה
למען אשר ישמור ה' על בריאות גופכם. החל מחדש תמוז אכלו ענבי-בוסר
למען ישולם רזון בגופכם ויצא מהם מנו השטן. בחדש אלול בצרו ענביכם
למען יש מש לכם עסיסם למשקה. ובחדש מרחסון - אספו את הצמוקים אשר
מלאך השמש המתיקם ויבשם, למען ירוח לגופכם בעוד שמלאכי האלהים
שוכנים בו. תאנים כבדות עסיס תאללו בחדשי אב ושבט ,וכל הנותר -
ישמרן עבורכם מלאכי-השמש. ואכלתם אותן עם שקדים של החדשים אשר אין
האילנת נושאים בהם פירות. ואת העשבים המופיעים לאחר הגשם אכלו
בחדש טבת למען יטהר דמכם מכל חטאיכם. ובחדש זה תחלו לאכול
גם מחלב בהמותיכם כי על כן נתן אלהים את עשב השדה לכל הבהמות החולבות
למען יזינו בחלבן בני אדם. כי באמונה אני אומר לכם: אשרי האיש
האוכל משלחנו של אלהים בלבד, ונמנע מכל תועבת השטן. אל תאכלו
מזונות טמאים המובאים מארצות רחוקות; אכלו תמיד רק מאשר נושאי
אילנותיכם. כי האלהים מיטיב לדעת מה טוב לגופכם ואימתי והיכן
והוא הנותן לכל האנשים בכל הממלכות את המזון הראוי להם."

"אַל תאכלו כעובדי כוכבים ומזלות המפטמים את עצמם בחפזה, בטמאם את
גופם בכל מיני מאכל פגול. כי ביודע עם המזון החי אשר אלהים מעניק לכם מעל
שלחנו המלכותי, יבוא בכם אונם של מלאכי האלהים. בשעת אכלכם ירחף עליכם
מלאך-האויר ולרגליכם ישב מלאך המים. ושאפתם ארוכות ועמוקות בכל
סעודותיכם למען יניעם לכם מלאך-האויר את האכילה; ולעשתם יפה-יפה את
המזון בטנכם עד שיהיה לנוזלים, כדי שמלאך המים יהפכנו בתוך גופכם
לדם. ואט-אט תאכלו, כמו שקועים היתם בתפלה לפני ה'. כי באמנה
אני אומר לכם: גבורת האלהים תבוא בקרבכם אם כה תסעדון ליד שלחנו.
בעוד שהשטן יהפוך לצמג מהביל את גופו של זה אשר מלאכי האויר והמים
אינם שורים בשעת סעודתו וה' ימאט בו מלשבת ליד שלחנו. כי כמזבח שלחן
ה' והסועד על שלחן אלהים הריהו כשרוי בהיכל. כי באמת אני אומר לכם:
גופם של בני האדם הופך להיכל וקרביהם – למזבח, אם מלא ימלאו את
מצוות האלהים; כי על כן אל לכם להטיל על המזבח כל דבר בשעת רוגזכם,
כן לא תהגו רעה באיש בעזמותכם בהיכלו של ה'. הכנסו איפוא לקדש הקדשים
של ה' רק בטעת רצון מלפני מלאכיו. באשר כל הנכס אוכלים בשעת
צער און זעם או בלא חשק, הופך לארס בגופכם. כי הבל פיו של השטן יטמאנו.
הקריבו בשמחה עולותיכם על מזבח-גופכם, וינוסו כל מחשבות און מתוך
לבבכם בשעה שהנכם קולסים לקרבכם את אונו של האל מעל שלחנו, ואל תשבו
אל שלחן אלהים בטרם יזמינכם באמצעות מלאך-התאבון."

"וְהַעֲנֵיג" איפוא, ליד השלחן המלכותי של מלאכי האלהים בחברתם, כי כן
תפיקו רצון מאת ה' וזכיתם לארך ימים על פני האדמה. באשר הטוב במשרתיו
ישרתכם אז כל הימים – הוא מלאך השמחה.

"וזכור תזכרו את היום השביעי שהוא קדש לה'. ששת ימים תזינו
גופכם במתנות ידה של אמא-אדמה, וביום השביעי קדשו גופכם לאביכם שבשמים
לא תאכלו ביום השביעי מזון גשמי כלשהו, ותחיו רק על דבר ה'. שהו כל
היום כלו בלוית מלאכי ה' במלכות האב שבשמים וביום השביעי יקימו
המלאכים את מלכות השמים בתוך גופכם כשם שהנכם עובדים ששת ימים במלכותה
של אמא-אדמה, ואל יפריע ביום השביעי מזון או פעולתם של המלאכים בתוך גופכם
ביום השביעי ויאריך ה' את חייכם על פני האדמה, למען תחיו חיי-נצח
במלכות השמים. כי באמנה אני אומר לכם: אם לא תסרור בכם יותר מחלה
על פני האדמה – תראו חיי נצח במלכות שדי.

"וְאלהים ישלח לכם מדי בקר את מלאך אור השמש להעירכם משנתכם, ואתם –
היענו להזמנת אביכם שבשמים ואל תוסיפו לשכב בעצלות על מטותיכם, כי
מלאכי האויר והמים כבר מצפים לכם בחוץ. והוו עמלים כל היום בעזרת
מלאכי-אמא-אדמה למען אשר תיטיבו להכיר ולדעת פעולתם יותר ויותר. אך
עם בוא השמש, כאשר אביכם שבשמים שולח לכם את מלאכו היקר מכל – הוא
מלאך השנה, אזי תפרשו לכם לנוח, ותשרו כל הלילה כולו עם מלאך השנה
ואביכם שבשמים ישלח לכם אז את מלאכיו הנעלמים למען יהיו עמכם במשך
הלילה הארוך. והמלאכים הנעלמים ילמדויכם דברים רבים ממלכות ה' כפי
שמלאכי אמא-אדמה הידועים לכם, מדריכים אותכם בדברים הנוגעים למלכותה.
כי באמת אני אומר לכם: לילה לילה תהיו אורחי מלכות אביכם שבשמים אם
תלכו במצוותיו, ומדי התעוררכם בבקר התחושו בקרבכם את אונם של המלאכים
הנעלמים. ואביכם שבשמים ישלחם אליכם מדי יום ביומו את מלאכיה על מנת
כפי שאמא-אדמה שולחת לכם מדי יום ביומו את מלאכיה על מנת מנת תעשות
יומם גופכם. כי באמנה אני אומר לכם: באם אמא-אדמה תחבקכם בזרועותיה
יומם – ואביכם שבשמים יעניק לכם את נשיקתו לילה – אזי יהיו בני האדר
לבני האלהים.

"דחו איפוא מעליכם יומם ולילה את פתויי השטן. אל תהיו ערים בלילה
ואל תישנו ביום, למען אשר לא יסטו אתכם מלאכי האלהים.

"אל תהנו עצמכם מטום משקאות ומכל קטורת עשן מאת השטן הנוזלים שנת
מעיניכם בלילה ומישעים אתכם ביום, כי באמת אני אומר לכם: כל המשקאות
וטמאשי העשן של השטן לתועבה הם בעיני אלהיכם.

"לא תנאפו בלילה או ביום, כי דומה הנואף לעץ אשר אשר ליחתו מחלחלת
מתוך גזעו והעץ ייבש טרם זמנו, אף לא יזכה לשאת פרי, על כן לא תנאפו
פן יוביש השטן את גופכם, וה' יעקר את זרעכם.

"המגעו מכל דבר חם מדי או קר מדי, כי זהו רצונה של אמכם-אדמה
לבל ינזק גופכם מן החום ומן הקור. ואל תניחו לגופכם שיחומם או
יצונן יותר מכפי שמלאכי האלהים מחממים או מצננים אותו. אם תלכו
במצרות אמכם-אדמה, והיה כל אימת שגופכם יתחמם למעלה מהמדה היא
תשלח את מלאך הצינה לצננכם, וכל אימת שגופכם יצטנן למעלה מהמדה
היא תשלח את מלאך החום לחממכם מחדש.

"עשר כדוגמת מלאכי האב שבשמים כולם, ושל אמא-אדמה הפועלים יומם
ולילה ללא הרף במלכויות השמים והארץ. על כן החדירו לקרבכם את
החזק שבמלאכי ה' - הוא מלאך הפעולה. ועבדתם כלכם בצוותא במלכות שדי.
עשו כדוגמת המים בזרמם, הרוח בנשבה, זריחת ובוא החמה, צמיחת הדשאים
והאילנות, החיות ברצון ובשקן, הירח בהתמעטו ובהתמלאו, הכוכבים
בזרחם ובהיעלמם. כל אלה נוע ינועו, ורק הדבר המת ידום. כי כל
אשר חיים באפו נוע ינוע - למים הוא. והאלהים הוא אלהי
החיים בעוד שהשטן - למתים הוא. עבדו איפוא את אל-חי למען שתנועת
החיים הנצחית תקיימכם ולמען תמלטו מן הדממה הנצחית של אבדון. עבדו
איפוא, ללא חשך, למען יצירת מלכות שדי, ולמען לא תפלו אל תחת שלשנו
של השטן, כי שמומו עולם שוררת במלכות האליטים בעדר שדומית-שממון
מאפילה על מלכות השאול של סטן. היו איפוא, בנים נאמנים לאמא-אדמה
ולאב שבשמים למען אשר לא תיהפכו לעבדי הסטן, ואמכם אדמה ומלאכיה
שבשמים ישלחו לכם את מלאכיהם ללמד, לאהוב, ולהרת אתכם, ומלאכיה
יחקקו את חוקי ה' במוחכם בלבכם ובידיכם למען אסר תדעון תרגישון
ותבצעון את חוקות האלהים.

"והתפללתם יום יום אל אביכם שבשמים ואמכם-אדמה, למען אשר תזהר
נסמתכם כאשר טהרו רוחו הקדושה של אביכם שבשמים ולמען יטהר גופכם
כגופה של אמא-אדמה, כי באם תבינו, תרגישו, ותעשו את המצוות, אזי
כל משאלותיכם מאת אביכם שבשמים ואמכם-אדמה - תנתנה לכם. כי חכמתו
אהבתו ויכלתו של הבורא עליונות על כל.

"וכה תתפללו לפני אביכם שבשמים: 'אבינו שבשמים, ישתבח שמך
תופיע מלכותך, יעש נא רצונך על האדמה כבמרום. תנה לנו ביום הזה
את לחם חוקנו ונחל נא לנו את חובותינו, כפי שאנו מוחלים לנעלי-
חובנו. ואל נא תעמידנו בנסיון, והושיענו מכל רע. כי לך המלכות
העז והגדולה לעולם ועד, אמן.

"וכה תתפללו לפני אמכם-אדמה: אמנו אשר על האדמה, ישתבח שמך,
תופיע מלכותך, ויקויים בנו רצונך כפי שהוא בך. כשם שהנך שולחת יום
יום את מלאכיך - שלוחים נא גם אלינו, כפרי לנו על עוונותינו כפי
שאנו מרחקים כל עוונותינו נגדך. אל תביאינו לידי מחלות והושיעינו
מכל רע, כי לך הארץ, הגוף, והבריאות אמן.
ויתפללו כולם יחד עם ישוע אל האל שבשמים ואל אמא-אדמה.

ולאחר הדברים האלה, דבר אליהם ישוע לאמור: " כשם סגופכם עשוי
להתחדש בידי מלאכי אמא-אדמה, כך יכולה רוחכם להתחדש בידי מלאכי האב
שבשמים. היו איפוא, בנים נאמנים לאביכם ולאמכם, ואחים נאמנים לבני
האדם. עד כה הייתם בריב עם אביכם ואמכם ואחיכם ותשרתו את השטן,
ומהיום והלאה, חיה חיו בשלום עם אביכם שבשמים, עם אמכם-אדמה ועם
אחיכם בני האדם ונלחמתם רק בשטן, לבל יגזול מכם את שלומכם. הנני
מוסר את שלום אמכם אדמה לגופכם ואת שלום אביכם שבשמים לרוחכם ויהי
נא שלום שניהם בין בני האדם. כל העיף והדואב והסובל - בואו אלי,
כי ברכת שלומי תעודדכם ותנחמכם. באשר ברכת שלומי רוויה אושר אין
קץ. כי על על כן הנני מברככם תדיר לאמור: "השלום עמכם!" כך ברכו נא
גם אתם איש אחיו למען אשר תפרוט אמכם-אדמה את סכת ומה על גופכם
ואביכם שבשמים יאציל את ברכת שלומו על רוחכם. אזי תמצאו את השלום
שרוי ביניכם, ומלביה שדי הכהן בקרבכם. ועתה חזרו לכם אל אחיכם אשר
עד עתה הייתם עמם בריב, ופרטו גם להם משלומכם, כי אסרי האיש המיחל
לשלום, באשר ינא ימצא את שלום ה'. לכו ואל תוסיפו לחטוא ופרשו
לכל אחד את שלומכם, כאשר נתתי אני את שלומי לכם. כי שלומי בא מעם
האלהים. השלום עמכם"... ויעזבם וילך. וינח שלומו עליהם, ובלבם
מלאך האהבה, ובראשם - בינת החוקים, ובידם - כוח ההתחדשות, ויבואו
בין בני האדם להביא את אור השלום לנאבקים באפלה.
ויפרדו ויאמרו איש לאחיו: "השלום עמם".

121

O that my words
Were graven with an iron pen
In the rock forever!
For I know that my Creator liveth:
And he shall stand at the end of time
Upon the earth and the stars.
And though worms destroy this body
Yet shall I see God.

                    —Thanksgiving Psalms

Book Three

LOST SCROLLS
OF THE ESSENE BROTHERHOOD

Now we have proudly separated ourselves from Nature, and the spirit of Pan is dead. Men's souls are scattered beyond the hope of unity, and the sword of formal creeds sharply separates them everywhere. To live in harmony with the Universe made life the performance of a majestic ceremony; to live against it was to creep aside into a *cul de sac*. Yet, even now, whispers of change are stealing over the face of the world once more. Like another vast dream beginning, man's consciousness is slowly spreading outwards once again. Some voice from the long ago is divinely trumpeting across our little globe. May this book carry it further! For the Gospel of the Essenes is indeed good tidings, pointing a way out of the dilemma of modern man.

E.B.S.

CONTENTS

PREFACE

Book Three

This third book of the Essene Gospel of Peace is a collection of texts of great spiritual, literary, philosophical and poetical value, created by two powerful, interwoven streams of tradition.

Chronologically, the first is the stream of traditions to which the Hebrew people were exposed in the Babylonian prison, dating from the Gilgamesh Epics to the Zend Avesta of Zarathustra. The second is the stream of traditions flowing with poetical majesty through the Old and New Testaments, dating from the ageless Énoch and the other Patriarchs, through the Prophets and on to the mysterious Essene Brotherhood.

In the buried library of the Essene Brotherhood at the Dead Sea, where the greatest number of scrolls were found, the texts of these two streams of traditions were very much interwoven. They follow each other in a strange succession: the powerful cubistic simplicity of the first juxtaposed with the majestic, expressionist poetry of the second.

The original texts of this collection may be classified into three approximate groups: about seventy percent of them are completely different from the ancient Sacred Books of the Avestas and the Old and New Testaments; twenty percent are similar, and ten percent are identical.

My desire in presenting this collection was to abstain from dry philological and exegetical interpretations, and instead to concentrate on their spiritual and poetical values, more attractive to twentieth century man. I tried to follow the style of my French translation of the first book of the Essene Gospel of Peace, which has now been published in seventeen languages, and has been distributed in over 200,000 copies.

I hope this Book Three will be as successful as Book One, and thus continue to bring these ageless inspirations to our disoriented century, guiding us, per secula seculorum, toward greater and greater light.

EDMOND BORDEAUX SZEKELY

INTRODUCTION

From the remote ages of antiquity a remarkable teaching has existed which is universal in its application and ageless in its wisdom. Fragments of it are found in Sumerian hieroglyphs and on tiles and stones dating back some eight or ten thousand years. Some of the symbols, such as for the sun, moon, air, water and other natural forces, are from an even earlier age preceding the cataclysm that ended the Pleistocene period. How many thousands of years previous to that the teaching existed is unknown.

To study and practice this teaching is to reawaken within the heart of every man an intuitive knowledge that can solve his individual problems and the problems of the world.

Traces of the teaching have appeared in almost every country and religion. Its fundamental principles were taught in ancient Persia, Egypt, India, Tibet, China, Palestine, Greece and many other countries. But it has been transmitted in its most pure form by the Essenes, that mysterious brotherhood which lived during the last two or three centuries B.C. and the first century of the Christian era at the Dead Sea in Palestine and at Lake Mareotis in Egypt. In Palestine and Syria the members of the brotherhood were known as Essenes and in Egypt as Therapeutae, or healers.

The esoteric part of their teaching is given in the Tree of Life, the Essene Communions with the Angels, and the Sevenfold Peace, among others. The exoteric or outer teaching appears in Book One of "The Essene Gospel of Peace" and the recently discovered Dead Sea Scrolls.

The origin of the brotherhood is said to be unknown, and the derivation of the name is uncertain. Some believe it comes from Esnoch, or Enoch, and claim him to be their founder, their Communions with the angelic world having first been given to him.

Others consider the name comes from Esrael, the elects of the people to whom Moses brought forth the Communions at Mount Sinai where they were revealed to him by the angelic world.

But whatever their origin, it is certain the Essenes existed for a very long time as a brotherhood, perhaps under other names in other lands.

The teaching appears in the Zend Avesta of Zarathustra, who translated it into a way of life that was followed for thousands of years. It contains the fundamental concepts of Brahmanism, the Vedas and the Upanishads; and the Yoga systems of India sprang from the same source. Buddha later gave forth essentially the same basic ideas and his sacred Bodhi tree is correlated with the Essene Tree of Life. In Tibet the teaching once more found expression in the Tibetan Wheel of Life.

The Pythagoreans and Stoics in ancient Greece also followed the Essene principles and much of their way of life. The same teaching was an element of the Adonic culture of the Phoenicians, of the Alexandrian School of Philosophy in Egypt, and contributed greatly to many branches of Western culture, Freemasonry, Gnosticism, the Kabala and Christianity. Jesus interpreted it in its most sublime and beautiful form in the seven Beatitudes of the Sermon on the Mount.

The Essenes lived on the shores of lakes and rivers, away from cities and towns, and practiced a communal way of life, sharing equally in everything. They were mainly agriculturists and arboriculturists, having a vast knowledge of crops, soil and climatic conditions which enabled them to grow a remarkable variety of fruits and vegetables in comparatively desert areas and with a minimum of labor.

They had no servants or slaves and were said to have been the first people to condemn slavery both in theory and practice. There were no rich and no poor amongst them, both conditions being considered by them as deviations from the Law. They established their own economic system, based wholly on the Law, and showed that all man's food and material needs can be attained without struggle, through knowledge of the Law.

They spent much time in study both of ancient writings and special branches of learning, such as education, healing and astronomy. They were said to be the heirs of Chaldean and Persian astronomy and the Egyptian arts of healing. They were adept in prophecy for which they prepared by prolonged fasting. In the use of plants and herbs for healing man and beast they were likewise proficient.

They lived a simple regular life, rising each day before sunrise to study and commune with the forces of nature, bathing in cold water as a ritual and donning white garments. After their daily labor in the fields and vineyards they partook of their meals in silence, preceding and ending them with prayer. In their profound respect for all living things they never touched flesh foods, nor did they drink fermented liquids. Their evenings were devoted to study and communion with the heavenly forces.

Evening was the beginning of their day, and their Sabbath, or holy day, began on Friday evening, the first day of their week. This day was given to study, discussion, the entertaining of visitors and the playing of certain musical instruments, relics of which have been discovered.

Their way of life enabled them to live to advanced ages of 120 years or more and they were said to have marvelous strength and endurance. In all their activities they expressed creative love.

They sent out healers and teachers from the brotherhoods, amongst whom were Elijah, John the Baptist, John the Beloved and the great Essene Master, Jesus.

Membership in the brotherhood was attainable only after a probationary period of a year and three years of initiatory work, followed by seven more years before being admitted to the full inner teaching.

Records of the Essene way of life have come down to us from the writings of their contemporaries. Pliny the Roman naturalist, Philo the Alexandrian philosopher, Josephus the Roman historian, Solanius and others, spoke of them variously as "a race by themselves, more remarkable than any other in the world," "the oldest of the initiates, receiving their teaching from Central Asia," "teaching perpetuated through an immense space of ages," "constant and unalterable holiness."

Some of the outer teaching is preserved in Aramaic text in the Vatican in Rome. Some in Slavic text was found in the possession of the Habsburgs in Austria and said to have been brought out of Asia in the thirteenth century by Nestorian priests fleeing the hordes of Genghis Khan.

Echoes of the teaching exist today in many forms, in certain rituals of the Masonic Order, in the symbol of the seven-branched candlestick, in the greeting "Peace be with you," used from the time of Moses, and even in the seven days of the week, which have long since lost their original spiritual meaning.

From its antiquity, its persistence through the ages, it is evident the teaching could not have been the concept of any individual or any people, but is the interpretation, by a succession of great Teachers, of the Law of the universe, the basic Law, eternal and unchanging as the stars in their courses, the same now as two or ten thousand years ago, and as applicable today as then.

The teaching explains the Law, shows how man's deviations from it are the cause of all his troubles, and gives the method by which he can find his way out of his dilemma.

THE SEVENFOLD VOW

I want to and will do my best
To live like the Tree of Life,
Planted by the Great Masters of our Brotherhood,
With my Heavenly Father,
Who planted the Eternal Garden of the Universe
And gave me my spirit;
With my Earthly Mother
Who planted the Great Garden of the Earth
And gave me my body;
With my brothers
Who are working in the Garden of our Brotherhood.

I want to and will do my best
To hold every morning my Communions
With the Angels of the Earthly Mother,
And every evening
With the Angels of the Heavenly Father,
As established by
The Great Masters of our Brotherhood.

I want to and will do my best
To follow the path of the Sevenfold Peace.

I want to and will do my best
To perfect my body which acts,
My body which feels,
And my body which thinks,
According to the Teachings
Of the Great Masters of our Brotherhood.

I will always and everywhere obey with reverence

My Master,
Who gives me the Light
Of the Great Masters of all times.

I will submit to my Master
And accept his decision
On whatever differences or complaints I may have
Against any of my brothers
Working in the Garden of the Brotherhood;
And I shall never take any complaint against a brother
To the outside world.

I will always and everywhere keep secret
All the traditions of our Brotherhood
Which my Master will tell me;
And I will never reveal to anyone these secrets
Without the permission of my Master.
I will never claim as my own
The knowledge received from my Master,
And I will always give credit to him
For all this knowledge.
I will never use the knowledge and power I have gained
Through initiation from my Master
For material or selfish purposes.

I enter the Eternal and Infinite Garden
With reverence to the Heavenly Father,
To the Earthly Mother, and
To the Great Masters,
Reverence to the Holy,
Pure and Saving Teaching,
Reverence to the Brotherhood of the Elect.

THE ESSENE WORSHIP

When God saw that his people would perish
Because they did not see the Light of Life,
He chose the best of Israel,
So that they might make the Light of Life
To shine before the sons of men,
And those chosen were called Essenes,
Because they taught the ignorant
And healed the sick,
And they gathered on the eve of every seventh day
To rejoice with the Angels.

WORSHIP

ELDER: Earthly Mother, give us the Food of Life!
BROTHERS: We will eat the Food of Life!
ELDER: Angel of Sun, give us the Fire of Life!
BROTHERS: We will perpetuate the Fire of Life!
ELDER: Angel of Water, give us the Water of Life!
BROTHERS: We will bathe in the Water of Life!
ELDER: Angel of Air, give us the Breath of Life!
BROTHERS: We will breathe the Air of Life!
ELDER: Heavenly Father, give us thy Power!
BROTHERS: We will build the Kingdom of God
*   with the Power of the Heavenly Father!*
ELDER: Heavenly Father, give us thy Love!
BROTHERS: We will fill our hearts with the Love
*   of the Heavenly Father!*
ELDER: Heavenly Father, give us thy Wisdom!
BROTHERS: We will follow the Wisdom

of the Heavenly Father!
ELDER: *Heavenly Father, give us Eternal Life!*
BROTHERS: *We will live like the Tree of Eternal Life!*
ELDER: *Peace be with thee!*
BROTHERS: *Peace be with thee!*

THE ANGEL OF SUN

Up! Rise up and roll along!
Thou immortal, shining,
Swift-steeded Angel of Sun!
Above the Mountains!
Produce Light for the World!

Angel of Sun, thou art the Fountain of Light:
Thou dost pierce the darkness.
Open thou the gate of the horizon!
The Angel of Sun doth dwell far above the earth,
Yet do her rays fill our days with life and warmth.
The chariot of the morning doth bring the light
Of the rising sun
And maketh glad the hearts of men.
The Angel of Sun doth illumine our path
With rays of splendor.
Angel of Sun!
Dart forth thy rays upon me!
Let them touch me; let them penetrate me!
I give myself to thee and thy embrace,
Blessed with the fire of life!
A molten flood of holy joy
Flows toward me from thee!
Onward to thee, Angel of Sun!
As no man can look upon the sun with naked eyes,
So no man can see God face to face,
Lest he be consumed by the flames
Which guard the Tree of Life.
Study, then, the Holy Law:
For the face of the Sun and the face of God

Can be seen only by the one who hath within him
The Revelation of the Law.
Thinkest thou that death is an end?
Thy thoughts are foolish as those of a child
Who sees dark sky and falling rain
And cries that there is no sun.
Wouldst thou grow strong in the Law?
Be, then, as the sun at noonday,
Which shineth with light and warmth on all men,
And giveth freely and abundantly of her golden glory.
Then shall the Fountain of Light flow back to thee,
As the Sun is never without light,
For it floweth freely, without restraint.
And when the Sun riseth,
Then the Earth, made by the Creator,
Becometh clean,
The running waters become pure,
The waters of the wells become pure,
The waters of the sea become pure,
The standing waters become pure,
All the Holy Creatures become pure.
It is through brightness and glory
That man is born who listens well
To the Holy Words of the Law,
Whom Wisdom holds dear.
Through their brightness and glory
Doth the Sun go his way,
Through their brightness and glory
Doth the Moon go her way,
Through their brightness and glory
Do the Stars go their way.
Unto the immortal, shining, swift-steeded Sun

Let there be invocation with sacrifice and prayer.
When the Light of the Sun waxeth brighter,
When the brightness of the Sun waxeth warmer,
Then do the heavenly forces arise.
They pour their Glory upon the Earth,
Made by the Heavenly Father,
For the increase of the Children of Light,
For the increase of the immortal,
Shining, swift-steeded Sun.
He who offers up a sacrifice
Unto the immortal, shining, swift-steeded Sun,
To withstand darkness,
To withstand death that creeps in unseen,
Offereth it up unto the Heavenly Father,
Offereth it up unto the Angels,
Offereth it up unto his own soul.
He rejoiceth all the heavenly and earthly forces
Who offereth up a sacrifice
Unto the immortal, shining, swift-steeded Sun.
I will sacrifice unto that friendship,
The best of all friendships,
That reign between the Angel of Sun
And the sons of the Earthly Mother.
I bless the Glory and Light,
The Strength and the Vigor,
Of the immortal, shining, swift-steeded Angel of Sun!

THE ANGEL OF WATER

From the Heavenly Sea
the Waters run and flow forward
from the never-failing Springs.

To the dry and barren desert
Have the Brothers brought the Angel of Water:
That she might bring forth a garden and a green place,
Tree-filled and fragrant with flowers.
Cast thyself into the enfolding arms
Of the Angel of Water:
For she shall cast out from thee
All that is unclean and evil.
Let my love flow toward thee, Heavenly Father,
As the river flows to the sea.
And let thy love flow to me, Heavenly Father,
As the gentle rain doth kiss the earth.
As a river through the forest
Is the Holy Law.
All creatures depend on it,
And it denieth nothing to any being.
The Law is to the world of men
What a great river is to streams and brooks.
As rivers of water in a dry place
Are the Brothers who bringeth the Holy Law
To the world of men.
In water mayest thou drown,
And in water mayest thou quench thy thirst.
Thus is the Holy Law a two-edged sword:
By the Law mayest thou destroy thyself,
And by the Law mayest thou see God.

Heavenly Father!
From thy Heavenly Sea flow all the Waters
That spread over all the seven Kingdoms.
This Heavenly Sea of thine alone
Goeth on bringing Waters
Both in summer and winter and in all seasons.
This Sea of thine purifieth the seed in males,
The womb in females,
The milk in female's breasts.
Thy Heavenly Sea floweth down unrestrained
Unto the big-seeded corn fields,
Unto the small-seeded pasture fields,
And unto the whole of the Earthly World.
A thousand pure Springs run toward the pastures
That give food to the Children of Light.
If any one shall sacrifice unto thee,
O thou holy Angel of Water!
To that one dost thou give both splendor and glory,
With health and with vigor of the body.
To him dost thou give a long enduring life,
And the Heavenly Sea, thereafter.
We worship all the holy waters
Which do quench the thirst of the earth,
All the holy waters that the Creator hath made,
And all the plants which the Creator hath made,
All of which are holy.
We do worship the Water of Life,
And all waters upon the earth,
Whether standing, or running, or waters of the well,
Or spring-waters which perennially flow,
Or the blessed drippings of the rains,
We do sacrifice unto the good and holy waters

Which the Law hath created.
Let the sea roar, and all the waters,
The world, and they that dwell therein.
Let the floods clap their hands,
Let the hills be joyful together.
The voice of the Lord is upon the waters:
The God of Glory thundereth.
Heavenly Father! and thou, Angel of Water!
We are thankful to thee, and we bless thy name.
A flood of love welleth up
From the hidden places beneath the earth:
The Brotherhood is blessed forever
In the Holy Water of Life.

THE ANGEL OF AIR

We worship the Holy Breath
Which is placed higher than
All the other things created;
And we worship
The most true Wisdom.

In the midst of the fresh air of the forest and fields,
There shalt thou find the Angel of Air.
Patiently she waits for thee
To quit the dank and crowded holes of the city.
Seek her, then, and quaff deeply
Of the healing draught which she doth offer thee.
Breathe long and deeply,
That the Angel of Air may be brought within you.
For the rhythm of thy breath is the key of knowledge
Which doth reveal the Holy Law.
The Angel of Air
Doth soar on invisible wings:
Yet thou must walk her unseen path
If thou wouldst see the face of God.
Sweeter than the finest nectar
Of honeyed pomegranate
Is the fragrance of the wind
In the grove of cypress.
Sweeter still the scent of the godly,
Who do revere and teach the Holy Law.
Holy is the Angel of Air,
Who doth cleanse all that is unclean
And giveth to all evil-smelling things a sweet odor.
Come on, come on, O clouds!

From above down on to the earth,
By thousands of drops,
Through their brightness and glory the winds blow,
Driving down the clouds
Toward the never-failing springs.
Vapors rise up from the vales of the mountains,
Pursued by the wind along the trail of the Law
Which increaseth the kingdom of Light.
The Heavenly Father hath made the earth by his power,
He hath established the world by his wisdom,
And hath stretched out the heavens by his will.
When he uttereth his voice,
There is a multitude of waters in the heavens,
And he causeth the vapors to ascend
From the ends of the earth;
He maketh lightnings with rain,
And bringeth forth the wind out of his breath.
As the sea is the gathering place of the waters,
Rising up and going down,
Up the aerial way and down on to the earth,
And up again the aerial way:
Thus rise up and roll along!
Thou for whose rising and growing
The Heavenly Father
Hath made the eternal and sovereign luminous Space.
No man may come before the Face of God
Whom the Angel of Air letteth not pass.
Thy body must breathe the air of the Earthly Mother,
As thy spirit must breathe the Holy Law
Of the Heavenly Father.

THE ANGEL OF EARTH

We invoke the Abundant Earth!
That possesseth Health and Happiness
And is more powerful
Than all its Creatures.

This wide earth do we praise,
Expanded far with paths,
The productive, the full-bearing,
Thy mother, holy plant!
We praise the lands where thou dost grow,
Sweet scented, swiftly spreading,
The good growth of the Earthly Mother.
We praise the good, the strong, the beneficent
Angel of Earth,
Who doth rejoice in the dew of heaven,
The fatness of the earth,
And the abundant harvest of corn and grapes.
We praise the high mountains,
Rich in pastures and in waters,
Upon which run the many streams and rivers.
We praise the holy plants of the Angel of Earth,
Which grow up from the ground,
To nourish animals and men,
To nourish the Children of Light.
The earth is the strong Preserver,
The holy Preserver, the Maintainer!
We praise the strength and vigor
Of the powerful Preserver, the earth,
Created by the Heavenly Father!
We praise the healers of the earth,

They who know the secrets of the herbs and plants;
To the healers hath the Angel of Earth
Revealed her ancient knowledge.
The Lord hath created medicines out of the earth,
And he that is wise shall use them.
Was not the water made sweet with wood,
That the virtue thereof might be known?
And to certain of the brothers he hath given skill,
That the Law might be honored and fulfilled.
With such do they heal men,
And taketh away their pains,
And of their works there is no end;
And from them is peace over all the earth.
Then give place to the healers, and honor them,
For the Heavenly Father hath created them:
Let them not go from thee, for thou hast need of them.
We praise the tillers of the soil,
Who work together in the Garden of the Brotherhood,
In the fields which the Lord hath blessed:
He who would till the earth,
With the left arm and with the right,
Unto him will she bring forth plenty of fruit,
And wholesome green plants and golden grain.
Sweetness and fatness will flow out from that land
And from those fields,
Along with health and healing,
With fulness and increase and plenty.
He who sows corn, grass and fruit
Soweth the Holy Law:
He maketh the Law of the Creator to progress.
When all the earth shall be a garden,
Then shall all the bodily world become free

From old age and death, from corruption and rot,
Forever and forever.
Mercy and truth shall be met together,
Righteousness and peace shall kiss each other,
Truth shall spring out of the earth,
And glory shall dwell in our land.

THE ANGEL OF LIFE

Be not ungrateful to thy Creator,
for he hath given thee Life.

Seek not the law in thy scriptures, for the law is Life,
Whereas the scriptures are only words.
I tell thee truly,
Moses received not his laws from God in writing,
But through the living word.
The law is living word of living God
To living prophets for living men.
In everything that is life is the law written.
It is found in the grass, in the trees,
In the river, in the mountains, in the birds of heaven,
In the forest creatures and the fishes of the sea;
But it is found chiefly in thyselves.
All living things are nearer to God
Than the scriptures which are without life.
God so made life and all living things
That they might by the everliving word
Teach the laws of the Heavenly Father
And the Earthly Mother
To the sons of men.
God wrote not the laws in the pages of books,
But in thy heart and in thy spirit.
They are in thy breath, thy blood, thy bone;
In thy flesh, thine eyes, thine ears,
And in every little part of thy body.
They are present in the air, in the water,
In the earth, in the plants, in the sunbeams,
In the depths and in the heights.

They all speak to thee
That thou mayest understand the tongue and the will
Of the living God.
The scriptures are the works of man,
But life and all its hosts are the work of God.
First, O Great Creator!
Thou didst create the Heavenly Powers
And thou didst reveal the Heavenly Laws!
Thou gavest unto us understanding
From thine own mind,
And thou madst our bodily life.
We are grateful, Heavenly Father,
For all thy manifold gifts of life:
For the precious things of heaven, for the dew,
For the precious fruits brought forth by the sun,
For the precious things put forth by the moon,
For the great things of the ancient mountains,
For the precious things of the lasting hills,
And for the precious things of the earth.
We are grateful, Heavenly Father,
For the vigor of health, health of the body,
Wise, bright and clear-eyed, with swiftness of foot,
Quick hearing of the ears, strength of the arms
And eye-sight of the eagle.
For all the manifold gifts of Life,
We do worship the Fire of Life,
And the Holy Light of the Heavenly Order.
We do worship the Fire,
The good and the friendly,
The Fire of Life!
The most beneficial and the most helpful,
The Fire of Life!

The most supporting, the most bountiful,
That Fire which is the House of the Lord!
Behold now the Child of Light
Who doth commune with the Angel of Life:
Lo now, his strength is in his loins,
And his force is in the muscles of his chest.
He moveth his legs like a cedar:
The sinews of his thighs are knit together.
His bones are as tubes of brass,
His limbs are like bars of iron.
He doth eat of the table of the Earthly Mother,
The grass of the field and the waters of the stream
Do nourish him;
Surely the mountains bring him forth food.
Blessed is his strength and beauty,
For he doth serve the Law.
A Sanctuary of the Holy Spirit
Is the body in which the Fire of Life
Doth burn with eternal Light.
We thank thee, Heavenly Father,
For thou hast put us at a source of running streams,
At a living spring in a land of drought,
Watering an eternal garden of wonders,
The Tree of Life, mystery of mysteries,
Growing everlasting branches for eternal planting
To sink their roots into the stream of Life
From an eternal source.

THE ANGEL OF JOY

The heavens smile, the earth celebrates,
the morning stars sing together,
and all the Children of Light shout for Joy.

O sing unto the Heavenly Father a new song:
Sing unto the Earthly Mother, all the earth.
Let the heavens rejoice, and let the earth be glad,
Let the sea roar, and the fulness of Eternal Life.
Let the field be joyful, and all that is therein:
Then shall all the trees of the wood
Rejoice before the Holy Law.
Sing unto the Heavenly Father,
All ye heavens of heavens,
And ye waters that be above the heavens,
All mountains and all hills,
Stormy wind fulfilling his word,
Fruitful trees and all cedars,
Beasts and all cattle,
Creeping things and flying fowl,
Kings of the earth and all people,
Princes and all judges of the earth:
Young men and maidens, old men and children,
Let them sing unto the Heavenly Father with Joy.
Sing unto the Lord with the harp, and voice of a psalm.
With trumpets and sound of pipes
Make a joyful noise before the Angels.
Let the floods clap their hands:
Let the hills be joyful together before the Lord.
Make a joyful noise unto the Lord, all ye lands.
Serve the Heavenly Father and the Earthly Mother

With gladness and joy:
Come before their presence with singing.
The spirit of the Holy Law is upon me,
Because the Elders have anointed me
To preach good tidings unto the meek.
They have sent me to bind up the brokenhearted,
To proclaim liberty to the captives,
And the opening of the prison to them that are bound;
To comfort all that mourn,
To send unto them the holy Angel of Joy,
To give unto them beauty for ashes,
The oil of joy for mourning,
The garment of Light for the spirit of heaviness,
For weeping may endure for a night,
But joy cometh in the morning.
The people that walked in darkness
Shall see a great light,
And they that dwell in the land of the shadow of death,
Upon them shall shine the light of the Holy Law.
Drop down, ye heavens, from above,
And let the skies pour down happiness.
Let the people of sadness go out with joy,
And be led forth with peace:
Let the mountains and the hills
Break forth before them into singing,
That they might partake of the holy celebration,
And eat of the fruit of the Tree of Life,
Which standeth in the Eternal Sea.
The sun shall be no more their light by day,
Neither for brightness
Shall the moon give light unto them:
But the Law shall be unto them an everlasting light,

And the Heavenly Father and the Earthly Mother
Shall be their eternal glory.
Their sun shall no more go down,
Neither shall their moon withdraw itself:
For the Law shall be their everlasting light,
And the days of their mourning shall be ended.
I will greatly rejoice in the Holy Law,
My soul shall be joyful in the Angels;
For they have clothed me in garments of light,
They have covered me with robes of joy.
As the earth bringeth forth her bud,
And as the garden causeth its seeds to spring forth,
So the Heavenly Father will cause the Holy Law
To spring forth with gladness and joy
Before all the Children of Light.
In the Garden of the Brotherhood,
All the earth shines with holiness and abundant joy,
For there are the seeds of the Holy Law sown.
The Law is the best of all good
For the Children of Light:
It giveth unto them brightness and glory,
Health and strength of the body,
Long life in communion with the Angels,
And eternal and unending Joy.
We will sing unto the Heavenly Father,
And unto the Earthly Mother,
And unto all the Angels,
As long as we live in the Garden of the Brotherhood:
We will sing praise unto the Holy Law
Forever and forever.

THE EARTHLY MOTHER

Honor thy Earthly Mother,
that thy days may be long upon the land.

Thy Earthly Mother is in thee, and thou in her.
She bore thee; she giveth thee life.
It was she who gaveth thee thy body,
And to her shalt thou one day give it back again.
Happy art thou when thou comest to know her
And her kingdom.
If thou receivest thy Mother's angels
And if thou doest her laws,
Who doeth these things shall never see disease.
For the power of our Mother is above all.
She hath rule over all the bodies of men
And all living things.
The blood which runs in us
Is born of the blood of our Earthly Mother.
Her blood falls from the clouds,
Leaps up from the womb of the earth,
Babbles in the brooks of the mountains,
Flows wide in the rivers of the plains,
Sleeps in the lakes,
Rages mightily in the tempestuous seas.
The air which we breathe
Is born of the breath of our Earthly Mother.
Her breath is azure in the heights of the heavens,
Soughs in the tops of the mountains,
Whispers in the leaves of the forest,
Billows over the cornfields,
Slumbers in the deep valleys,

Burns hot in the desert.
The hardness of our bones
Is born of the bones of our Earthly Mother,
Of the rocks and of the stones.
They stand naked to the heavens
On the tops of the mountains,
They are as giants that lie sleeping
On the sides of the mountains,
As idols set in the desert,
And are hidden in the deepness of the earth.
The tenderness of our flesh
Is born of the flesh of our Earthly Mother,
Whose flesh waxeth yellow and red
In the fruits of the trees,
And nurtures us in the furrows of the fields.
The light of our eyes,
The hearing of our ears,
Both are born of the colors and sounds
Of our Earthly Mother;
Which enclose us about
As the waves of the sea a fish,
As the eddying air a bird.
Man is the Son of the Earthly Mother,
And from her did the Son of Man
Receive his whole body,
Even as the body of the newborn babe
Is born of the womb of his mother.
Thou art one with the Earthly Mother;
She is in thee, and thou in her.
Of her wert thou born, in her dost thou live,
And to her shalt thou return again.
Keep, therefore, her laws,

For none can live long, neither be happy,
But he who honors his Earthly Mother
And doeth her laws.
For thy breath is her breath,
Thy blood her blood,
Thy bone her bone,
Thy flesh her flesh,
Thy eyes and thy ears,
Are her eyes and her ears.
Our Earthly Mother!
Always are we embraced by her,
Always are we surrounded by her beauty.
Never can we part from her;
Never can we know her depths.
Ever doth she create new forms:
That which now existeth never was before.
That which did exist returneth not again.
In her kingdom all is ever new, and always old.
In her midst do we live, yet we know her not.
Continually doth she speak to us,
Yet never doth betray to us her secrets.
Ever do we till her soil and harvest her crops,
Yet we have no power over her.
Ever doth she build, ever doth she destroy,
And her workplace is hidden from the eyes of men.

THE ANGEL OF POWER

Thine, O Heavenly Father!
was the Power, when thou didst order
a Path for each of us and all.

What is the Deed well done?
It is that done by the Children of Light
Who regard the Law as before all other things.
The best of all gifts, therefore,
Do I beseech of thee, O thou best of beings,
Heavenly Father!
That the Holy Law shall rule within us
Through thy Angel of Power!
I do approach thee with my invocations,
That thy great gifts of power
Will protect thy Heavenly Order,
And thy creative mind within us, forever.
We will extol thee, Heavenly Father,
O almighty king!
And we will bless thy power forever and ever.
So long as we be able and may have the power,
So long will we teach the people
Concerning these Deeds to be done by them
With faith toward the Heavenly Father,
The Earthly Mother, the holy Angels,
And all the Children of Light
Who till the soil of the Garden of the Brotherhood,
And in the desire for the coming of the Heavenly Order
Into their souls and their bodies.
Thine, O Heavenly Father! was the Power,
Yea, thine, O Creator of Love!

Was the understanding and the spirit,
When thou didst order a path for each of us and all.
Through thy Power shall we go unto the people,
And teach them, saying, Trust in the Law,
And walk in the ways of the holy Angels,
So shalt thou dwell in the land,
And verily thou shalt be fed from the feast table
Of the Earthly Mother.
Delight thyself also in the Power
Of the Heavenly Father,
And he shall give thee the desires of thine heart.
Let not arrogancy come out of thy mouth:
For the Heavenly Father doth rule by the holy Law,
And by him actions are weighed.
He bringeth down to the grave, and bringeth up.
The Power of the Law maketh poor, and maketh rich:
His Power bringeth low, and lifteth up.
He raiseth up the poor out of the dust,
And lifteth up the beggar from the dunghill,
And maketh them inherit the throne of glory.
Out of heaven shall he thunder
Upon the children of darkness:
The Lord shall judge with Power the ends of the earth.
Hear the voices of the Brothers
Who cry out in the wilderness and barren desert:
Prepare ye the way of the Law,
Make straight the paths of the Heavenly Father,
And the Earthly Mother,
And all the holy Angels of the day and of the night.
Every valley shall be filled,
And every mountain and hill shall be brought low;
And the crooked shall be made straight,

And the rough ways shall be made smooth,
And all flesh shall see the Power of the Law.
We extol thee, Heavenly Father,
For thou hast lifted us up.
O Lord, our Almighty Powerful Father,
We cried unto thee, and thou hast healed us.
From the grave thou hast brought up
The souls of the people;
Thou hast kept them alive,
That they should not go down to the pit.
O Heavenly Father, thou art the Law;
Early and late will we seek thy Angels:
Our souls thirsteth for the Law,
Our flesh longeth for the Law.
A river of holy Power is the Law
In a dry and thirsty land, where no water is.
Our lips shall praise thy Power while we live,
We will lift up our hands in thy name.
We will preserve, we will nurture thy Heavenly Order
Through the fulfillment of Deeds.
We will invoke and pronounce by day and by night
Thy holy Power,
And that Power shall come to help us;
It will be as if there were a thousand angels
Watching over one man.
Unto thee, Heavenly Father, belongeth all Power,
And also unto thee belongeth mercy:
For the holy Law doth render to every man
According to his work.

THE ANGEL OF LOVE

Love is stronger
than the currents of deep waters.
Love is stronger than death.

Beloved, let us love one another:
For love is of the Heavenly Father:
And every one that loveth is born
Of the Heavenly Father and the Earthly Mother,
And knoweth the Angels.
Ye shall love one another,
As the Heavenly Father hath loved you.
For the Heavenly Father is love:
And he that dwelleth in love
Dwelleth in the Heavenly Father,
And the Heavenly Father in him.
Let him that love him be as the sun
When he goeth forth in his might.
Brothers, be ye all of one mind,
Having endless love and compassion one for another.
Thou shalt not avenge, nor bear any grudge
Against the children of thy people,
But thou shalt love thy neighbor as thyself.
If a man say,
I love the Heavenly Father, but hate my brother,
He is a liar:
For he that loveth not his brother whom he hath seen,
How can he love the Heavenly Father
Whom he hath not seen?
He who loveth the Heavenly Father
Loveth also his brother.

Love ye also the stranger:
For ye were strangers in the land of Egypt.
It is said by the people,
Better a dinner of herbs where love is,
Than a stalled ox and hatred therewith.
Loving words are as an honeycomb,
Sweet to the soul, and health to the bones.
The words of a man's mouth are as deep waters,
And the wellspring of love as a flowing brook.
What doth the Law require of thee,
But to do justly, and to love mercy,
And to walk humbly with the Angels.
By this do we know that the Angel of Love
Doth dwell in us,
When we love the Heavenly Father,
And keep his Law.
O Gracious Love!
O Creator of Love!
Reveal the best words
Through thy divine mind living within us.
Say to the Children of Light
Who till the soil in the Garden of the Brotherhood:
Honor all men.
Love the Brotherhood.
Obey the Law.

THE ANGEL OF WISDOM

To follow the Lord
Is the beginning of Wisdom:
And the knowledge
Of the Holy One
Is understanding.
For by him
Thy days shall be multiplied,
And the years of thy life
Shall be increased.

All Wisdom cometh from the Heavenly Father,
And is with him forever.
Through the holy Law doth the Angel of Wisdom
Guide the Children of Light.
Who can number the sand of the sea,
And the drops of rain, and the days of eternity?
Who can find out the height of heaven,
And the breadth of the earth,
And the deep, and wisdom?
Wisdom hath been created before all things.
One may heal with goodness,
One may heal with justice,
One may heal with herbs,
One may heal with the Wise Word.
Amongst all the remedies,
This one is the healing one
That heals with the Wise Word.
This one it is that will best drive away sickness
From the bodies of the faithful,
For Wisdom is the best healing of all remedies.
To follow the holy Law is the crown of Wisdom,

Making peace and perfect health to flourish,
Both which are the gifts of the Angels.
We would draw near unto thee, O Heavenly Father!
With the help of thy Angel of Wisdom,
Who guides us by means of thy Heavenly Order,
And with the actions and the words
Inspired by thy holy Wisdom!
Come to us, Heavenly Father, with thy creative mind,
And do thou, who bestoweth gifts
Through thy Heavenly Order,
Bestow alike the long-lasting gift of Wisdom
Upon the Children of Light,
That this life might be spent in holy service
In the Garden of the Brotherhood.
In the realm of thy good mind,
Incarnate in our minds,
The path of Wisdom doth flow
From the Heavenly Order,
Wherein doth dwell the sacred Tree of Life.
In what fashion is manifest thy Law,
O Heavenly Father!
The Heavenly Father makes answer:
By good thought
In perfect unity with Wisdom,
O Child of Light!
What is the word well spoken?
It is the blessing-bestowing word of Wisdom.
What is the thought well thought?
It is that which the Child of Light thinketh,
The one who holdeth the Holy Thought
To be the most of value of all things else.
So shall the Child of Light grow

In concentration and communion,
That he may develop Wisdom,
And thus shall he continue
Until all the mysteries of the Infinite Garden
Where standeth the Tree of Life
Shall be revealed to him.
Then shall he say these victorious words:
O Heavenly Father!
Give unto me my task
For the building of thy Kingdom on earth,
Through good thoughts, good words, good deeds,
Which shall be for the Child of Light
His most precious gift.
O thou Heavenly Order!
And thou Universal Mind!
I will worship thee and the Heavenly Father,
Because of whom the creative mind within us
Is causing the Imperishable Kingdom to progress!
Holy Wisdom maketh all men free from fear,
Wide of heart, and easy of conscience.
Holy Wisdom, the understanding that unfolds forever,
Continually, without end,
And is not acquired through the holy scrolls.
It is ignorance that ruineth most people,
Both amongst those who have died,
And those who shall die.
When ignorance will be replaced by Holy Wisdom,
Then will sweetness and fatness come back again
To our land and to our fields,
With health and healing,
With fulness, and increase, and growth,
And abundance of corn and of grass,
And rivers of Peace shall flow through the desert.

And Enoch walked with God;
and he was not; for God took him.

Upon the earth was no man created like Enoch,
For he was taken from the earth.
He was as the morning star in the midst of a cloud,
And as the moon at the full:
As the sun shining upon the temple of the most High,
And as the rainbow giving light in the bright clouds,
And as the flower of roses in the spring of the year,
As lilies by the rivers of waters,
And as the branches of the frankincense tree
In the time of summer,
And as a fair olive tree budding forth fruit,
And as a cypress tree which groweth up to the clouds.
The first follower of the Law was Enoch,
The first of the healers, of the wise,
The happy, the glorious, the strong,
Who drove back sickness and drove back death.
He did obtain a source of remedies
To withstand sickness and to withstand death;
To withstand pain and to withstand fever;
To withstand the evil and infection
Which ignorance of the Law
Had created against the bodies of mortals.
We invoke Enoch,
The master of life,
The Founder of our Brotherhood,
The man of the Law,
The wisest of all beings,

The best ruling of all beings,
The brightest of all beings,
The most glorious of all beings,
The most worthy of invocations amongst all beings,
The most worthy of glorification amongst all beings,
Who first thought what is good,
Who first spoke what is good,
Who first did what is good.
Who was the first Priest,
The first Plougher of the Ground,
Who first knew and first taught the Word,
And the obedience to the Holy Law.
To all the Children of Light
He gave all the good things of life:
He was the first bearer of the Law.
It is written, the words of Father Enoch:
We sacrifice unto the Creator,
The Heavenly Father,
The bright and glorious Angels.
We sacrifice unto the shining heavens,
We sacrifice unto the bright, all-happy, blissful wisdom
Of the Holy Angels of Eternity.
Grant to us, Heavenly Father!
The desire and the knowledge of the straightest path,
The straightest because of the Heavenly Order of Life,
The Best Life of the Angels,
Shining, all glorious.
As health is excellent, so also is Eternal Life,
Both flowing from the Heavenly Order,
The creator of goodness of the mind,
And of actions of life performed for devotion
To the Creator of Eternal Life.

We sacrifice unto the sovereign sky,
We sacrifice unto the boundless time,
We sacrifice unto the endless sea of Eternal Life.
We do invoke the most glorious Law.
We invoke the Kingdom of Heaven,
The boundless time, and the Angels.
We invoke the eternal, holy Law.
We follow the paths of the Stars,
The Moon, the Sun and the endless Light,
Moving around in their revolving circle forever.
And truthfulness in Thought, Word and Deed
Will place the soul of the faithful man
In the endless light of Eternal Life.
The Heavenly Father possessed me
In the beginning of his way, before his works of old.
I was set up from everlasting, from the beginning,
Or ever the earth was.
When there were no depths, I was brought forth:
While as yet he had not made the earth, nor the fields,
Nor the beginning of the dust of the world.
When he established the heavens, I was there:
When he set a circle upon the face of the deep:
When he made firm the skies above:
When the fountain of the deep became strong:
When he gave to the sea its bound,
That the waters should not transgress his Law:
When he marked out the foundations of the earth:
Then I was by him, as a master workman:
And I was daily his delight,
Rejoicing always before him,
Rejoicing in his habitable earth,
And my delight was with the sons of men.

For eternity the Heavenly Father reigneth,
He is clothed with majesty and strength.
He is from everlasting!
The floods have lifted up, O Lord,
The floods have lifted up their voice,
The floods lift up their waves.
The Heavenly Father on high
Is mightier than the noise of many waters,
Yea, than the mighty waves of the sea.
His name shall endure forever,
His name shall be continued as long as eternity,
And all the Children of Light shall be blessed in him,
And all men shall call him blessed.
Let the whole earth be filled
With the glory of the Heavenly Father,
The Earthly Mother,
And all the holy Angels.
I have reached the inner vision
And through thy spirit in me
I have heard thy wondrous secret.
Through thy mystic insight
Thou hast caused a spring of knowledge
To well up within me,
A fountain of power, pouring forth living waters,
A flood of love and of all-embracing wisdom
Like the splendor of Eternal Light.

THE ANGEL OF WORK

Who hath measured the waters
In the hollow of his hand,
And meted out heaven with a span,
And comprehended the dust of the earth
In a measure,
And weighed the mountains in scales,
And the hills in a balance?

The sun ariseth, and the Brothers gather together,
They go forth unto their work in the fields;
With strong backs and cheerful hearts they go forth
To labor together in the Garden of the Brotherhood.
They are the Workers of Good,
Because they work the good of the Heavenly Father.
They are the spirit, conscience and soul of those
Who teach the Law and who struggle for the Law.
With the right arm and the left, they till the soil,
And the desert bursts forth in colors of green and gold.
With the right arm and the left, they lay the stones
Which shall build on earth the Kingdom of Heaven.
They are the messengers of the Angel of Work:
In them is revealed the holy Law.
O Heavenly Father! How manifold are thy works!
In wisdom hast thou made them all;
The earth is full of thy riches.
Thou sendest the springs into the valleys,
Which run among the hills.
Thou givest drink to every beast of the field,
And causeth the grass to grow for the cattle.
Thou settest the mighty trees in their places,

That the birds of heaven may have their habitation,
And sing sweetly among the branches.
Thou givest herbs for the service of man,
That he may bring forth food out of the earth.
In the hands of the Brothers all thy gifts bear fruit,
For they are building on earth the Kingdom of Heaven.
Thou openest thine hand, they are filled with good.
Thou sendest forth thy spirit, they are created,
And together with thy holy Angels,
They shall renew the face of the earth.
O thou Heavenly Father!
Thou who art one alone!
Reveal unto the Children of Light:
Which is the foremost place
Wherein the earth feeleth the greatest joy?
The Heavenly Father answering, said:
It is the place whereupon one of the Brothers
Who follow the holy Law, steppeth forth:
With his good thoughts, good words and good deeds!
Whose back is strong in service,
Whose hands are not idle,
Who lifteth up his voice in full accord with the Law.
That place is holy whereon one of the Brothers
Soweth the most of corn, of grass, of fruit:
Where he watereth that ground which is dry,
Or draineth the too wet soil.
For the earth hath been given unto the keeping
Of the Children of Light,
That they treasure and care for it,
And bring from its depths only that
Which is for the nourishment of the body.
Blessed are the Children of Light

Whose joy is in the work of the Law,
Who labor in the Garden of the Brotherhood by day,
And join the Angels of the Heavenly Father by night.
From their lips is the story told,
Which doth serve as a teaching for the sons of men:
It is said that the trees went forth on a time
To anoint a king over them;
And they said unto the olive tree,
"Reign thou over us."
But the olive tree said unto them,
"Should I leave my fatness,
Wherewith by me they honor God and man,
And go to be promoted over the trees?"
And the trees said to the fig tree,
"Come thou, and reign over us."
But the fig tree said unto them,
"Should I forsake my sweetness, and my good fruit,
And go to be promoted over the trees?"
Then said the trees unto the vine,
"Come thou, and reign over us."
And the vine said unto them,
"Should I leave my wine,
Which cheereth God and man,
And go to be promoted over the trees?"
The man of the Law who fulfills his tasks
Does not need further blessings.

THE ANGEL OF PEACE

For the earth shall be filled
with the Peace of the Heavenly Father,
as the waters cover the sea.

\

I will invoke the Angel of Peace,
Whose breath is friendly,
Whose hand is clothed in power.
In the reign of Peace, there is neither hunger nor thirst,
Neither cold wind nor hot wind,
Neither old age nor death.
In the reign of Peace,   .
Both animals and men shall be undying,
Waters and plants shall be undrying,
And the food of life shall be never-failing.
It is said that the mountains
Shall bring peace to the people,
And the little hills, righteousness.
There shall be peace
As long as the sun and moon endure,
Throughout all generations.
Peace shall come down like rain upon mown grass,
As showers that water the earth.
In the reign of Peace shall the Law grow strong,
And the Children of Light shall have dominion
From sea to sea, unto the ends of the earth.
The reign of Peace hath its source
In the Heavenly Father;
By his strength he setteth fast the mountains,
He maketh the outgoings of morning and evening
To rejoice in the Light,

He bringeth to earth the river of the Law,
To water and enrich it,
He maketh soft the earth with showers;
They drop upon the pastures of the wilderness,
And the little hills rejoice on every side.
The pastures are clothed with flocks;
The valleys also are covered over with corn;
They shout for joy, they also sing.
O Heavenly Father!
Bring unto thy earth the reign of Peace!
Then shall we remember the words
Of him who taught of old the Children of Light:
I give the peace of thy Earthly Mother
To thy body,
And the peace of thy Heavenly Father
To thy spirit.
And let the peace of both
Reign among the sons of men.
Come to me all that are weary,
And that suffer in strife and affliction!
For my peace will strengthen thee and comfort thee.
For my peace is exceeding full of joy.
Wherefore do I always greet thee after this manner:
Peace be with thee!
Do thou always, therefore, so greet one another,
That upon thy body may descend
The Peace of thy Earthly Mother,
And upon thy spirit
The Peace of thy Heavenly Father.
And then wilt thou find peace also among thyselves,
For the Kingdom of the Law is within thee.
And return to thy Brothers

And give thy peace to them also,
For happy are they that strive for peace,
For they will find the peace of the Heavenly Father.
And give to every one thy peace,
Even as I have given my peace unto thee.
For my peace is of God.
Peace be with thee!

THE HEAVENLY FATHER

In the Heavenly Kingdom
There are strange and wondrous works,
For by his word all things consist.
There are yet hid greater things than these be,
For we have seen but a few of his works:
The Heavenly Father hath made all things.

The beauty of heaven, the glory of the stars,
Give light in the highest places of the Heavenly Sea.
Sentinels of the most High, they stand in their order,
And never faint in their watches.
Look upon the rainbow, and praise him that made it;
Very beautiful it is in the brightness thereof.
It compasseth the heaven about with a glorious circle,
And the hands of the most High have bended it.
By his Law he maketh the snow to fall apace,
And sendeth swiftly the lightnings of his judgment.
Through this the treasures are opened,
And clouds fly forth as fowls.
By his great power he maketh the clouds firm,
And the hailstones are broken small.
At his sight the mountains are shaken,
And at his will the south wind bloweth.
The noise of the thunder maketh the earth to tremble:
So doth the northern storm and the whirlwind:
As birds flying he scattereth the snow,
And the eye marvelleth
At the beauty of the whiteness thereof,
And the heart is astonished at the raining of it.
So do the heavens declare the glory of God,

And the firmament showeth his handiwork.
Who hath made the waters,
And who maketh the plants?
Who to the wind hath yoked the storm-clouds,
The swift and even the fleetest?
Who, O Heavenly Father,
Is the creator of the holy Law within our souls?
Who hath made the light and the darkness?
Who hath made sleep and the zest of the waking hours?
Who gave the recurring sun and stars
Their undeviating way?
Who established that whereby the moon doth wax
And whereby she waneth?
Who, save thee, Heavenly Father,
Hath done these glorious things!
Lord, thou hast been our dwelling place
In all generations.
Before the mountains were brought forth,
Or ever thou hadst formed the earth and the world,
Even from everlasting to everlasting, thou art the Law.
Thy name is Understanding,
Thy name is Wisdom,
Thy name is the Most Beneficent,
Thy name is the Unconquerable One,
Thy name is He Who maketh the true account,
Thy name is the All-seeing One,
Thy name is the Healing One,
Thy name is the Creator.
Thou art the Keeper,
Thou art the Creator and the Maintainer;
Thou art the Discerner and the Spirit.
Thou art the Holy Law.

These names were pronounced
Before the Creation of this Heaven,
Before the making of the waters and of the plants,
Before the birth of our holy Father Enoch.
Before the beginning of time,
The Heavenly Father planted the holy Tree of Life,
Which standeth forever in the midst of the Eternal Sea.
High in its branches sings a bird,
And only those who have journeyed there,
And have heard the mysterious song of the bird,
Only those shall see the Heavenly Father.
They shall ask of him his name,
And he shall answer, I am that I am,
Being ever the same as the Eternal I am.
O thou Heavenly Father!
How excellent is thy name in all the earth!
Thou hast set thy glory above the heavens.
When we consider thy heavens, the work of thy fingers,
The moon and the stars, which thou hast ordained,
What is man, that thou art mindful of him?
Yet thou hast made a covenant
With the Children of Light,
And they walk with thy holy Angels;
Thou hast crowned them with glory and honor,
Thou madest them to have dominion
Over the works of thy hands,
And gavest unto them
The task of nourishing and protecting
All that lives and grows on thy green earth.
O Heavenly Father!
How excellent is thy name in all the earth!
Hear the voice of one who cries out to thee:

Whither shall I go from thy spirit?
Or whither shall I flee from thy presence?
If I ascend up into heaven, thou art there;
If I make my bed in hell, behold, thou art there.
If I take the wings of the morning,
And dwell in the uttermost parts of the sea,
Even there shall thy hand lead me,
And thy right hand shall hold me.
If I say, "Surely the darkness shall cover me,"
Even the night shall be light about me;
Yea, the darkness hideth not from thee
But the night shineth as the day:
The darkness and the light are both alike to thee,
For thou hast possessed my reins.
As the hart panteth after the water brooks,
So panteth my soul after thee, O God.
My soul thirsteth for the living Heavenly Father.
The Law is my light and salvation;
Whom shall I fear?
The Law is the rock and the strength of my life;
Of whom shall I be afraid?
One thing have I desired of the Law,
That I will seek after:
That I may dwell in the house of the Law
All the days of my life,
To behold the beauty of the Heavenly Father.
Those who dwell in the secret place of the most High
Shall abide under the shadow of the Almighty.
We will say of the Law,
"Thou art our refuge and our fortress;
We will trust in the Holy Law."
And the Heavenly Father

Shall cover us with his feathers,
And under his wings shall we trust;
His truth shall be our shield and buckler.
We shall not be afraid for the terror by night,
Nor for the arrow that flieth by day,
Nor for the pestilence that walketh in darkness,
Nor for the destruction that wasteth at noonday.
For by day we shall walk
With the Angels of the Earthly Mother,
By night we shall commune
With the Angels of the Heavenly Father,
And when the sun reacheth its zenith at noontide,
We shall stand silent before the Sevenfold Peace:
And no evil shall befall us,
Neither shall any plague come nigh our dwelling,
For he hath given his Angels charge over us,
To keep us in all their ways.
The Heavenly Father is our refuge and strength.
Therefore will not we fear,
Though the earth be removed,
And though the mountains be carried
Into the midst of the sea,
Though the waters thereof roar and be troubled,
Though the mountains shake with the swelling thereof.
There is a river, which floweth to the Eternal Sea.
Beside the river stands the holy Tree of Life.
There doth my Father dwell, and my home is in him.
The Heavenly Father and I are One.

THE HOLY LAW

Thou, O Holy Law,
The Tree of Life
That standeth in the middle
Of the Eternal Sea,
That is called,
The Tree of Healing.
The Tree of powerful Healing,
The Tree of all Healing,
And upon which rests the seeds
Of all we invoke.

Have ye not known? have ye not heard?
Hath it not been told thee from the beginning?
Lift up thine eyes on high, and behold the Holy Law,
Which was established before the eternal,
Sovereign and luminous space,
Which hath created the foundations of the earth,
Which is the first and the last,
Which liveth in the hearts of the Children of Light.
For the Law is great,
As the Heavenly Father is great above his Angels:
He it is who giveth us the Law, and he is the Law:
In his hand are the deep places of the earth;
The strength of the hills is his also.
The sea is his, and he made it,
And his hands formed the dry land.
Come, let us worship and bow down,
Let us kneel before the Heavenly Father,
For he is the Law,
And we are the people of his pasture,
And the sheep of his hand.

With songs of gladness the Children of Light
Invoke the Holy Law:
Sickness flies away before it,
Death flies away,
Ignorance flies away.
Pride, scorn and hot fever,
Slander, discord and evil,
All anger and violence,
And lying words of falsehood,
All fly away before the power of the Holy Law.
Here is the Law
Which will smite all sickness,
Which will smite all death,
Which will smite the oppressors of men,
Which will smite pride,
Which will smite scorn,
Which will smite hot fevers,
Which will smite all slanders,
Which will smite all discords,
Which will smite the worst of evil,
Which will banish ignorance from the earth.
We bless the invocation and prayer,
The strength and vigor of the Holy Law.
We invoke the spirit, conscience and soul
Of the Children of Light who teach the Law,
Who struggle in the kingdom of darkness
To bring the light of the Law to the sons of men.
We bless that victory
Of good thoughts, good words, and good deeds,
Which make strong the foundations
Of the Kingdom of Light.
Let the sons of men who think, speak and do

All good thoughts, words and deeds
Inhabit heaven as their home.
And let those who think, speak and do
Evil thoughts, words and deeds
Abide in chaos.
Purity is for man, next to life,
The greatest of good:
That purity is in the Holy Law,
Which maketh grass to grow upon the mountains,
And maketh clean the hearts of men.
With good thoughts, good words, and good deeds
Clean shall be the fire,
Clean the water,
Clean the earth,
Clean the stars, the moon and the sun,
Clean the faithful man and the faithful woman,
Clean the boundless, eternal Light,
Clean the Kingdom of the Earthly Mother
And the Kingdom of the Heavenly Father,
Clean the good things made by the Law,
Whose offspring is the Holy Creation.
To obtain the treasures of the material world,
O sons of men,
Forego not the world of the Law.
For he who, to obtain the treasures
Of the material world,
Destroyeth in him the world of the Law,
Such an one shall possess neither force of life
Nor the Law,
Neither the Celestial Light.
But he who walks with the Angels,
And who followeth the Holy Law,

He shall obtain everything good:
He shall enter the Eternal Sea
Where standeth the Tree of Life.
The Communions of the Law are perfect,
Converting the soul from darkness to light;
The testimony of the Law is sure,
Making wise the simple.
The statutes of the Law are right, rejoicing the heart;
The commandment of the Law is pure,
Enlightening the eyes.
The truth of the Law is clean, enduring forever.
Let the Children of Light triumph everywhere
Between the Heavens and the Earth!
Let us breathe the Holy Law in our prayer:
How beautiful are thy tabernacles,
O Heavenly Father!
My soul longeth, yea, even fainteth
For the Tree of Life
That standeth in the middle of the Eternal Sea.
My heart and my flesh crieth out for the living God.
Yea, the sparrow hath found a house,
And the swallow a nest for herself,
Where she may lay her young.
The Children of Light
Who labor in the Garden of the Brotherhood
Abide in the Holy Law:
Blessed are they who dwell therein!

THE ANGELS

The Heavenly Father
Gave his Angels charge
Concerning thee:
And in their hands
They shall bear thee up,
Even unto the Tree of Life
That standeth in the midst
Of the Eternal Sea...

For the wisdom of the Law,
For the unconquerable power of the Law,
And for the vigor of health,
For the Glory of the Heavenly Father
And the Earthly Mother,
And for all the boons and remedies
Of the Sevenfold Peace,
Do we worship the Holy Angels,
Our efforts for whom
And Communions to whom
Make us good in the eyes of Heavenly Father.
The Law is fulfilled according to the Angels,
The Bright and Holy Ones,
Whose looks perform their wish,
Strong, lordly,
Who are undecaying and holy,
Who are seven and seven all of one Thought,
Who are seven and seven all of one Speech,
Who are seven and seven all of one Deed.
Whose Thought is the same,
Whose Speech is the same,
Whose Deed is the same,

Whose Father is the same,
Namely, the Heavenly Father!
The Angels who see one another's souls,
Who bring the Kingdom of the Earthly Mother
And the Kingdom of the Heavenly Father
To the Children of Light
Who labor in the Garden of the Brotherhood.
The Angels who are the Makers and Governors,
The Shapers and Overseers,
The Keepers and Preservers of the abundant Earth!
And of all Creations of the Heavenly Father.
We invoke the good, the strong, the beneficent
Angels of the Heavenly Father and the Earthly Mother!
That of the Light!
That of the Sky!
That of the Waters!
That of the Earth!
That of the Plants!
That of the Children of Light!
That of the Eternal Holy Creation!
We worship the Angels
Who first listened unto the thought and teaching
Of the Heavenly Father,
Of whom the Angels formed the seed of the nations.
We worship the Angels
Who first touched the brow of our Father Enoch,
And guided the Children of Light
Through the seven and seven Paths
Which lead to the Tree of Life
That standeth forever in the midst of the Eternal Sea.
We worship all the Angels,
The good, heroic and bounteous Angels,

Of the bodily world of the Earthly Mother,
And those of the Invisible Realms,
Those in the Celestial Worlds of the Heavenly Father.
We worship the ever blessing immortal Angels,
The brilliant ones of splendorous countenance,
The lofty and devoted creatures of the Heavenly Father,
They who are imperishable and Holy.
We worship the resplendent, the glorious,
The bountiful Holy Angels,
Who rule aright, and who adjust all things rightly.
Hear the glad voices of the Children of Light,
Who sing the praise of the Holy Angels
As they labor in the Garden of the Brotherhood:
We sing with gladness to the waters, land and plants,
To this earth and to the heavens,
To the holy wind, and the holy sun and moon,
To the eternal stars without beginning,
And to all the holy creatures of the Heavenly Father.
We sing with gladness unto the Holy Law,
Which is the Heavenly Order,
To the days and to the nights,
To the years and to the seasons
Which are the pillars of the Heavenly Order.
We worship the Angels of the Day,
And the Angels of the Month,
Those of the Years, and those of the Seasons,
All the good, the heroic,
The ever blessing immortal Angels
Who maintain and preserve the Heavenly Order.
We desire to approach the mighty Angels,
All the Angels of the Heavenly Order,
Because of the Holy Law,

Which is the best of all good.
We do present these thoughts well thought,
These words well spoken,
These deeds well done,
To the bountiful, immortal Angels,
Those who exercise their right rule.
We do present these offerings
To the Angels of the Day,
And the Angels of the Night,
The ever-living, the ever-helpful,
Who dwell eternally with the Divine Mind.
May the good and heroic and bountiful
Angels of the Heavenly Father
And the Earthly Mother
Walk with their holy feet
In the Garden of the Brotherhood,
And may they go hand in hand with us
With the healing virtues of their blessed gifts,
As wide-spread as the earth,
As far-spread as the rivers,
As high-reaching as the sun,
For the furtherance of the betterment of man,
And for abundant growth.
It is they, the Holy Angels,
Who shall restore the World!
Which will thenceforth never grow old and never die!
Never decaying, ever living and ever increasing.
Then Life and Immortality will come
And the World will be restored!
Creation will grow deathless,
The Kingdom of the Heavenly Father will prosper,
And evil shall have perished!

Behold, how good and how pleasant it is
For the Children of Light
To dwell together in unity!
For the Brotherhood
The Heavenly Father
Hath commanded the Law.
Even life for evermore.

The Law was planted in the Garden of the Brotherhood
To illumine the hearts of the Children of Light,
To make straight before them
The seven and seven paths leading to the Tree of Life
Which standeth in the midst of the Eternal Sea;
The Law was planted in the Garden of the Brotherhood,
That they might recognize
The spirits of truth and falsehood,
Truth born out of the spring of Light,
Falsehood from the well of darkness.
The dominion of all the Children of Truth
Is in the hands of the mighty angels of Light,
So that they walk in the ways of Light.
The Children of Light are the servants of the Law,
And the Heavenly Father shall not forget them.
He hath blotted out their sins as a thick cloud;
He hath lit the candle of Truth within their hearts.
Sing, O ye heavens,
Shout, ye lower parts of the earth,
Break forth into singing, ye mountains,
O forest, and every tree therein:
For the Heavenly Father hath kindled his flame

In the hearts of the Children of Light,
And glorified himself in them.
The Holy Law of the Creator
Purifieth the followers of the Light
From every evil thought, word and deed,
As a swift-rushing mighty wind
Doth cleanse the plain.
Let the Child of Light who so desireth
Be taught the Holy Word,
During the first watch of the day and the last,
During the first watch of the night and the last,
That his mind may be increased in intelligence
And his soul wax strong in the Holy Law.
At the hour of dawn
He shall gaze upon the rising sun
And greet with joy his Earthly Mother.
At the hour of dawn
He shall wash his body in the cool water
And greet with joy his Earthly Mother.
At the hour of dawn
He shall breathe the fragrant air
And greet with joy his Earthly Mother.
And through the day
He shall labor with his brethren
In the Garden of the Brotherhood.
In the hour of twilight
He shall gather with his brothers,
And together they shall study the holy words
Of our fathers, and their fathers' fathers,
Even unto the words of our Father Enoch.
And when the stars are high in the heavens
He shall commune

With the holy Angels of the Heavenly Father.
And his voice shall be raised with gladness
Unto the most High, saying,
We worship the Creator,
The maker of all good things:
The Good Mind,
And of the Law,
Immortality,
And the Holy Fire of Life.
We do offer to the Law
The Wisdom of the Tongue,
Holy Speech, Deeds, and rightly-spoken Words.
Grant us, Heavenly Father,
That we may bring down abundance
To the world thou hast created,
That we may take away both hunger and thirst
From the world thou hast created,
That we may take away both old age and death
From the world thou hast created.
O good, most beneficent Heavenly Father!
Grant us that we may think
According to the Law,
That we may speak
According to the Law,
That we may do
According to the Law.
O Heavenly Father,
What is the invocation most worthy
In greatness and goodness?
It is that one, O Children of Light,
That one delivers
When waking up and rising from sleep,

At the same time professing
Good thoughts, good words and good deeds,
And rejecting evil thoughts, evil words and evil deeds.
The first step
That the soul of the Child of Light did make,
Placed him in the Good Thought Paradise,
The Holy Realm of Wisdom.
The second step
That the soul of the Child of Light did make,
Placed him in the Good Word Paradise,
The Holy Realm of Love.
The third step
That the soul of the Child of Light did make,
Placed him in the Good Deed Paradise,
The Holy Realm of Power.
The fourth step
That the soul of the Child of Light did make,
Placed him in the Endless Light.
The Heavenly Father knoweth the hearts
Of the Children of Light,
And their inheritance shall be for ever.
They shall not be afraid in the evil time:
And in the days of famine they shall be satisfied.
For with them is the Fountain of Life,
And the Heavenly Father forsaketh not his children.
Their souls shall breathe forever and ever,
And their forms shall be endowed with Eternal Life.
Blessings on the Children of Light
Who have cast their lot with the Law,
That walk truthfully in all their ways.
May the Law bless them with all good
And keep them from all evil,

And illumine their hearts
With insight into the things of life
And grace them with knowledge of things eternal.

TREES

Go towards the high growing Trees,
And before one of them
Which is beautiful, high growing and mighty,
Say thou these words:
Hail be unto Thee!
O good living Tree,
Made by the Creator.

In the days of old, when the Creation was young,
The earth was filled with giant trees,
Whose branches soared above the clouds,
And in them dwelled our Ancient Fathers,
They who walked with the Angels,
And who lived by the Holy Law.
In the shadow of their branches all men lived in peace,
And wisdom and knowledge was theirs,
And the revelation of the Endless Light.
Through their forests flowed the Eternal River,
And in the center stood the Tree of Life,
And it was not hidden from them.
They ate from the table of the Earthly Mother,
And slept in the arms of the Heavenly Father,
And their covenant was for eternity with the Holy Law.
In that time the trees were the brothers of men,
And their span on the earth was very long,
As long as the Eternal River,
Which flowed without ceasing
From the Unknown Spring.
Now the desert sweeps the earth with burning sand,
The giant trees are dust and ashes,

And the wide river is a pool of mud.
For the sacred covenant with the Creator
Was broken by the sons of men,
And they were banished from their home of trees.
Now the path leading to the Tree of Life
Is hidden from the eyes of men,
And sorrow fills the empty sky
Where once the lofty branches soared.
Now into the burning desert
Come the Children of Light,
To labor in the Garden of the Brotherhood.
The seed they plant in the barren soil
Will become a mighty forest,
And trees shall multiply
And spread their wings of green
Until the whole earth be covered once again.
The whole earth shall be a garden,
And the tall trees shall cover the land.
In that day shall sing the Children of Light a new song:
My brother, Tree!
Let me not hide myself from thee,
But let us share the breath of life
Which our Earthly Mother hath given to us.
More beautiful than the finest jewel
Of the rugmaker's art,
Is the carpet of green leaves under my bare feet;
More majestic than the silken canopy
Of the rich merchant,
Is the tent of branches above my head,
Through which the bright stars give light.
The wind among the leaves of the cypress
Maketh a sound like unto a chorus of angels.

Through the rugged oak and royal cedar
The Earthly Mother hath sent a message of Eternal Life
To the Heavenly Father.
My prayer goeth forth unto the tall trees:
And their branches reaching skyward
Shall carry my voice to the Heavenly Father.
For each child thou shalt plant a tree,
That the womb of thy Earthly Mother
Shall bring forth life,
As the womb of woman doth bring forth life.
He who doth destroy a tree
Hath cut off his own limbs.
Thus shall sing the Children of Light,
When the earth again shall be a garden:
Holy Tree, divine gift of the Law!
Thy majesty reunites all those
Who have strayed from their true home,
Which is the Garden of the Brotherhood.
All men will become brothers once again
Under thy spreading branches.
As the Heavenly Father hath loved all his children,
So shall we love and care for the trees
That grow in our land,
So shall we keep and protect them,
That they may grow tall and strong,
And fill the earth again with their beauty.
For the trees are our brothers,
And as brothers,
We shall guard and love one another.

STARS

The white, shining,
Far seen Stars!
The piercing, health-bringing,
Far piercing Stars!
Their shining rays,
Their brightness and glory
Are all, through thy Holy Law,
The Speakers of thy praise,
O Heavenly Father!

Over the face of heaven
Did the Heavenly Father hurl his might:
And lo! He did leave a River of Stars in his wake!
We invoke the bright and glorious Stars
That wash away all things of fear
And bring health and life unto all Creations.
We invoke the bright and glorious Stars
To which the Heavenly Father
Hath given a thousand senses,
The glorious Stars that have within themselves
The Seed of Life and of Water.
Unto the bright and glorious Stars
Do we offer up an Invocation:
With wisdom, power and love,
With speech, deeds and rightly-spoken words,
Do we sacrifice unto the bright and glorious Stars
That fly towards the Heavenly Sea
As swiftly as the arrow
Darteth through heavenly Space.
We invoke the bright and glorious Stars,

That stand out beautiful,
Spreading comfort and joy
As they commune within themselves.
The Holy Works,
The Stars, the Suns, and the many-colored Dawn
Which bringeth on the Light of Days,
Are all, through their Heavenly Order,
The Speakers of thy praise,
O thou great giver, the Holy Law!
We invoke the Lord of the Stars,
The Angel of Light,
The ever-awake!
Who taketh possession
Of the beautiful, wide-expanding Law,
Greatly and powerfully,
And whose face looketh over
All the seven and seven Kingdoms of the Earth;
Who is swift amongst the swift,
Bountiful amongst the bounteous,
Strong amongst the strong,
The Giver of Increase,
The Giver of Sovereignty,
The Giver of Cheerfulness and Bliss.
We invoke the Lord of the Stars,
The Angel of Light,
Who is truth-speaking,
With a thousand ears and ten thousand eyes,
With full knowledge, strong and ever-awake.
The Heavenly Order pervades all things pure,
Whose are the Stars,
In whose Light the glorious Angels are clothed.
Great is our Heavenly Father, and of great power:

His understanding is infinite.
He telleth the number of the stars;
He calleth them all by their names.
Behold the height of the stars!
How high they are!
Yet the Heavenly Father doth hold them in his palms,
As we do sift the sand in ours.
He who knoweth not the Holy Law
Is as a wandering star
In the darkness of an unknown sky.
Thinkest thou there is but one way
To see the firmament?
Suppose ye the stars were but broken places in the sky
Through which the glory of heaven is revealed
In fragments of blazing light!
In the purple night
Traversed by the continual Stars
Shall the souls of the Children of Light
Take wing and join the Angels of the Heavenly Father.
Then shall the Eternal Sea
Reflect the shining glory of the heavens,
And the branches of the Tree of Life reach to the Stars.
Then shall the Kingdom of Heaven
Fill all the earth with Glory,
And the shining Stars of the most High
Shall blaze within the hearts of the Children of Light
And warm and comfort the seeking sons of men.

THE MOON

Unto the luminous Moon
Which keepeth within itself
The seed of many species,
Let there be invocation
With sacrifice and prayer...

When the Light of the Moon waxeth warmer,
Golden hued plants grow up from the earth
During the season of Spring.
We sacrifice unto the New Moons
And unto the Full Moons;
The crescent of the New Moon is full of holy Peace:
We sacrifice unto the Angel of Peace.
The radiant and luminous Moon
Keepeth within itself the seed:
The bright, the glorious,
The water-giving,
The warmth-giving,
The wisdom-giving,
The thoughtfulness-giving,
The freshness-giving,
The healing one, the Moon of Peace!
With silent and peace-giving light
The Moon doth shine
Upon the pastures, the abodes,
The waters, the lands and the plants
Of our earthly garden.
The Moon and the Sun,
The holy Wind and the Stars without beginning,
Self-determined and self-moved,

All are regulators of the Holy Order,
Of the days and nights,
Of the months and years.
The face of the Moon doth change its aspect,
Yet is ever the same:
As the Holy Law doth reveal a different face
To each of the Children of Light,
Yet is unchanged in its Essence.
We invoke the New Moon and the Moon that is waning,
And the Full Moon that scattereth the Night,
And the yearly festivals and the seasons
Of the Heavenly Father.
For it was he who gavest the moon
Her increase and her decrease,
That through her we might know the movements
Of the day and of the night.
Thou silver and luminous moon!
We are grateful that we may look on thee,
And see in thy reflection
The blessed face of our Earthly Mother.
Among the world of the sons of men,
The Brothers of Light are flames of radiance,
As the stars pale in the presence
Of the bright and shining moon.
The moon walketh in brightness across the sky,
And delight in the Holy Law doth fill our hearts.
Peace, Peace, Peace,
Holy Angel of Peace,
Illumine the silver moon with thy holiness,
That all may look upon its beauty
And feel thy eternal Peace.
The desert sky is blue with night,

And we see the first ray of the New Moon,
Chaste and beautiful.
Then do the Brothers greet one another
With love and thanksgiving,
Saying, "Peace be with thee!
Peace be with thee!"

I am grateful, Heavenly Father,
For thou hast raised me to an eternal height,
And I walk in the wonders of the plain.
Thou gavest me guidance
To reach thine eternal company
From the depths of the earth.
Thou hast purified my body
To join the army of the angels of the earth
And my spirit to reach
The congregation of the heavenly angels.
Thou gavest man eternity
To praise at dawn and dusk
Thy works and wonders
In joyful song.

O all ye works of the Heavenly Order,
Bless ye the Law:
Praise and exalt the Law above all for ever.
O ye heavens, bless ye the Law:
Praise and exalt the Law above all for ever.
O ye Angels of the Heavenly Father,
And ye Angels of the Earthly Mother,
Bless ye the Law:
Praise and exalt the Law above all for ever.
O all ye waters that be above the heavens,
Bless ye the Law.
O all ye powers of the Holy Angels, bless ye the Law.
O ye sun and moon, bless ye the Law.
O ye stars of heaven, bless ye the Law.
O every shower and dew, bless ye the Law.
O all ye winds, bless ye the Law.

O ye fire and heat, bless ye the Law.
O ye winter and summer, bless ye the Law.
O ye light and darkness, bless ye the Law.
O ye dews and storms of snow, bless ye the Law.
O ye nights and days, bless ye the Law.
O ye lightnings and clouds, bless ye the Law.
O ye mountains and little hills, bless ye the Law.
O all ye things that grow on the earth, bless ye the Law.
O ye fountains, bless ye the Law.
O ye seas and rivers, bless ye the Law.
O ye whales, and all that move in the waters,
Bless ye the Law.
O all ye fowls of the air, bless ye the Law.
O all ye beasts and cattle, bless ye the Law.
O ye children of men, bless ye the Law.
O ye spirits and souls of the Children of Light,
Bless ye the Law.
O ye holy and humble workers
In the Garden of the Brotherhood, bless ye the Law.
O let the whole earth bless the Law!
O give thanks unto the Heavenly Father,
And bless ye his Law.
O all ye that worship the Law,
Give praise unto the Heavenly Father
And the Earthly Mother,
And all the Holy Angels,
And give unto them thanks,
For the Law endureth for ever.
We worship the Law by day and by night.
Hail to the Heavenly Father!
Hail to the Earthly Mother!
Hail to the Holy Angels!

Hail to the Children of Light!
Hail to our holy Father Enoch!
Hail to the whole of Holy Creation
That was, that is, or ever shall be!
We sacrifice unto the bright and glorious stars,
We sacrifice unto the sovereign sky,
We sacrifice unto boundless time,
We sacrifice unto the good Law
Of the worshipers of the Creator,
Of the Children of Light
Who labor in the Garden of the Brotherhood;
We sacrifice unto the way of the Holy Law.
We sacrifice unto all the Holy Angels
Of the world unseen;
We sacrifice unto all the Holy Angels
Of the material world.
O give thanks unto the Heavenly Father, for he is good,
O give thanks unto the God of the Angels,
O give thanks unto the Lord of Light,
For his mercy endureth for ever.
To him who alone doeth great wonders,
To him that by wisdom made the heavens,
To him that stretched out the earth above the waters,
To him that made great lights in the heavens,
To him that made the sun to rule by day,
And the moon and stars to rule by night,
Give unending praise and thanksgiving,
For his mercy endureth for ever.
And we do worship the ancient and holy religion,
Which was instituted at the Creation,
Which was on the earth in the time of the Great Trees;
The holy religion of the Creator,

The resplendent and the glorious,
Revealed unto our Father Enoch.
We do worship the Creator,
And the Fire of Life,
And the good Waters which are Holy,
And the resplendent Sun and the Moon,
And the lustrous, glorious Stars;
And most of all we do worship the Holy Law,
Which the Creator, our Heavenly Father,
Hath given to us.
It is the Law which maketh holy our dwelling place,
Which is the wide green earth.
Praise ye the Law!
The Law healeth the broken in heart,
And bindeth up their wounds.
Great is the Law, and of great power;
The understanding of the Law is infinite.
The Law lifteth up the meek,
And casteth the wicked down to the ground.
Sing unto the Law with thanksgiving,
Sing praise upon the harp unto the Law,
Which covereth the heaven with clouds,
Which prepareth rain for the earth,
Which maketh grass to grow upon the mountains.
We praise aloud the well-thought Thought,
The Word well-spoken,
And the Deed well-done.
We will come to thee, O ye bountiful immortals!
We will come to thee, extolling and invoking thee,
Angels of the Heavenly Father and the Earthly Mother!
We do worship the Holy Lord of the Heavenly Order,
The Creator of all good creatures of the earth.

And we do worship the utterances of our Father Enoch,
And his ancient, pure religion,
His faith and his lore, older than the beginning of time.
We will sing unto the Law as long as we live,
We will sing praise unto our Heavenly Father
While we have our being,
While the Garden of the Brotherhood doth endure.
Our Communions with the Angels shall be sweet;
We will be glad in the Law.
Bless thou the Law, O my soul.
Praise ye the Holy Law.
The Children of Light love the Law,
Because the Law heareth our voices
And our supplications.
An all-hearing ear hath the Law inclined unto us,
Therefore will we call upon the Law as long as we live.
The Law hath delivered our souls from death,
Our eyes from tears, and our feet from falling.
We will walk before the Law in the land of the living:
In the paths of the Infinite Garden of the Brotherhood.
The days of the sons of men are as grass;
As flowers of the field, so they flourish.
For the wind passeth over them, and they are gone:
But the mercy of the Law is from everlasting
To everlasting upon them that follow it.
Bless the Heavenly Father, all ye his Angels;
Ye ministers of his, that do his pleasure.
Bless the Lord, all his works,
In all places of his dominion:
Bless the Lord, O my soul.
O Heavenly Father, thou art very great!
Thou art clothed with honor and majesty.

Who coverest thyself with light as with a garment,
Who stretchest out the heavens like a curtain,
Who layeth the beams of his chambers in the waters,
Who maketh the clouds his chariot,
Who walketh upon the wings of the wind,
Who maketh his Angels spirits,
His Children of Light a flaming fire
To kindle the Truth in the hearts of the sons of men,
Who laid the foundations of the earth.
Bless the Heavenly Father, O my soul!

LAMENTS

Out of the depths have I cried unto thee, O Lord.
Lord, hear my voice!

Hear my prayer, O Lord,
And let my cry come unto thee.
Hide not thy face from me
In the day when I am in trouble;
Incline thine ear unto me;
In the day when I call answer me speedily.
For my days are consumed like smoke,
And my bones are burned as a hearth.
My heart is smitten, and withered like grass;
So that I forget to eat my bread.
By reason of the voice of my groaning
My bones cleave to my skin.
I am like a pelican of the wilderness;
I am like an owl of the desert.
I watch, and am as a sparrow,
Alone upon the house top.
My days are like a shadow that declineth;
And I am withered like grass.
O my God, take me not away in the midst of my days:
The heavens are the work of thy hands.
They shall perish, but thou shalt endure.
The first step taken
By the soul of the wicked man,
Laid him in the evil thought hell.
The second step take
By the soul of the wicked man,
Laid him in the evil word hell.

The third step taken
By the soul of the wicked man,
Laid him in the evil deed hell.
The fourth step taken
By the soul of the wicked man,
Laid him in endless darkness.
I know that thou canst do all things,
And that no purpose of thine can be restrained.
Now mine eye seeth thee,
Wherefore I abhor myself,
And repent in dust and ashes.
For the wicked sons of men
Have sinned against themselves,
And their hell of evil thoughts, evil words and evil deeds
Is a hell of their own making.
But my anguish and my bitter tears
Are for our ancient fathers,
Who sinned against the Creator,
And were banished
From the Holy Kingdom of the Great Trees.
Wherefore I weep, and hide my face in sorrow,
For the beauty of the Lost Garden,
And the vanished sweetness of the song of the Bird,
Who sang in the branches of the Tree of Life.
Have mercy upon me, O God,
And cleanse me from my sin.
The joy of our hearts is ceased,
Our dance is turned into mourning.
The crown is fallen from our head:
Woe unto us, that we have sinned!
For this our heart is faint,
For these things our eyes are dim.

Thou, O Heavenly Father, remainest for ever,
Thy throne from generation to generation.
Wherefore dost thou forget us for ever,
And forsake us so long time?
Turn thou us unto thee, O Lord,
Renew our days as of old.
Where there is no righteousness or compassion,
There wild beasts of the desert shall lie;
And their houses shall be full of doleful creatures.
And owls shall dwell there,
And satyrs shall dance there.
And the wild beasts shall cry in their desolate houses.
Wash me, O Lord, and I shall be whiter than snow.
Make me to hear joy and gladness;
Hide thy face from my sins,
And blot out all mine iniquities.
Create in me a clean heart, O God;
And renew a right spirit within me.
Cast me not away from thy presence;
And take not thy holy spirit from me.
Restore unto me the joy of thy Infinite Garden,
And uphold me with thy Holy Angels.
Let me drive away all evil things
And all uncleanness,
From the fire, the water,
The earth, the trees,
From the faithful man and the faithful woman,
From the stars, the moon, the sun,
From the boundless Light,
And from all good things,
Made by thee, O Heavenly Father,
Whose offspring is the Holy Law.

By the rivers of Babylon,
There we sat down, yea, we wept,
When we remembered Zion.
We hanged our harps upon the willows.
How shall we sing the Lord's song
In a wicked land?
If I forget thee, O Jerusalem,
Let my right hand forget her cunning.
If I do not remember thee,
Let my tongue cleave to the roof of my mouth;
For Babylon is the slavery in the world,
And Zion is the freedom in the Brotherhood.
O Lord, to thee will I cry!
For the fire hath devoured the pastures
Of the wilderness,
And the flame hath burned
All the trees of the field.
The beasts of the field cry also unto thee:
For the rivers of waters are dried up,
And the fire hath devoured
The pastures of the wilderness.
Let all the inhabitants of the land tremble:
For the day of the Lord cometh,
For it is nigh at hand;
A day of darkness and gloominess,
A day of clouds and of thick darkness,
A day when the earth shall quake,
And the heavens shall tremble.
The sun and the moon shall be dark,
And the stars shall withdraw their shining.
Out of the depths will we cry unto thee, O Lord!
Lord, hear thou our voices!

Hearken unto me, my people,
And give ear unto me!
Lift up thine eyes to the heavens,
And look upon the earth beneath:
For the heavens shall vanish away like smoke,
And the earth shall wax old like a garment,
And they that dwell therein
Shall die in like manner:
But my Kingdom shall be for ever,
And my Law shall not be abolished.

And in that day hell shall enlarge herself,
And open her mouth without measure:
And the glory, the pride and the pomp of the wicked
Shall descend into it.
And the mean man shall be brought down,
And the mighty man shall be humbled,
As the fire devoureth the stubble,
And the flame consumeth the chaff;
So their root shall be as rottenness,
And their blossom shall go up as dust.
Because they have cast away
The Holy Law of the Heavenly Order,
And despised the word of the Children of Light.
And in that day, one will look unto the land
And behold only darkness and sorrow,
And the light in the heavens shall be darkened.
The leaders of the people shall cause them to err,
And they that are led of them shall be destroyed.
For every one is an hypocrite and an evil doer,

And every mouth speaketh folly.
Wickedness burneth as the fire:
It shall devour the briars and thorns.
It shall kindle in the thickets of the forest,
And shall mount up like the lifting up of smoke.
Through the wrath of the Law
Shall the land be darkened,
For this hath man wrought upon himself.
And the people shall be as the fuel of the fire:
No man shall spare his brother.
Woe unto them that have kept not the Holy Law!
Woe unto the crown of pride!
Woe unto those who lust after the things of the world,
And corrupt themselves with wrongdoing,
Who err in vision, and stumble in judgment:
For they are a rebellious people, a lying people,
People who will not hear the Law of the Lord:
Which say to the seers, see not,
And to the Prophets, prophesy not unto us right things,
But speak unto us smooth things, prophesy deceits.
Woe unto them that decree unrighteous decrees,
And that write grievousness which they have prescribed.
Woe unto them that join house to house,
That lay field to field,
Till there be no place that a man may be alone
In the midst of the earth!
Woe unto them that rise up early in the morning,
Not to commune with the Angels,
But to follow strong drink, and continue until night,
Till the fumes of the wine inflame them!
Woe unto them that call evil good, and good evil,
That put darkness for light, and light for darkness.

Woe unto them
That turn aside the needy from judgment,
And take away the right from the poor,
That make of widows their prey, and rob the fatherless!
Wherefore it shall come to pass
That the hand of the Lord shall lop the bough
With the judgment of the Law,
And the high ones of stature shall be hewn down
And the haughty shall be humbled.
Howl ye, for the day of the Law is at hand;
It shall come as a destruction from the Almighty.
Therefore shall all hands be faint,
And every man's heart shall melt.
And they shall be afraid:
Pangs and sorrows shall take hold of them;
They shall be in pain as a woman that travaileth:
They shall be amazed one at another:
Their faces shall be as flames.
Behold, the day of the Lord cometh,
Cruel both with wrath and fierce anger,
To lay the land desolate:
And he shall destroy the sinners thereof out of it.
It shall come to pass in that day,
That the Lord shall punish the host of the high ones,
And the kings of the earth upon the earth.
And they shall be gathered together,
As prisoners are gathered in the pit,
And shall be shut up in the prison.
And the Lord shall come forth out of his place,
And will come down,
And tread upon the high places of the earth.
And the mountains shall be molten under him,

And the valleys shall be cleft, as wax before the fire,
As the waters pour down a steep place.
Then the moon shall vanish, and the sun be obscured.
And the stars of heaven and the constellations thereof
Shall not give their light:
The sun shall be darkened in its going forth,
And the moon shall not cause her light to shine.
And the Lord will shake the heavens,
And the earth shall remove out of her place,
In the day of the wrath of the Law,
In the day of the fierce anger of the Lord.
And the shining cities shall be laid waste,
And wild beasts of the desert shall lie there;
The hay shall wither away, the grass shall fail,
And in all the earth there shall be no green thing.
In that day shall the strong cities
Be as a forsaken bough,
And a tempest of hail
Shall sweep away the refuge of lies,
And the angry waters
Shall overflow the hiding place of the wicked.
And there shall be upon every high mountain,
And upon every high hill,
Rivers and streams of waters
In the day of the great slaughter,
When the towers fall.
In that day shall the light of the moon
Be as the light of the sun,
And the light of the sun shall be sevenfold.
Behold, the name of the Law cometh from far,
Burning with hot anger,
And the burden thereof is heavy:

The lips of the Lord are full of indignation,
And his tongue is as a devouring fire.
He shall show the strength of his arm,
With the flame of consuming fire,
With scattering, and tempest, and hailstones.
The land shall be utterly emptied, and utterly spoiled,
For the sons of men have turned away from the Law.
The city of confusion is broken down:
Every house is shut up, that no man may come in.
There is a crying and wailing in the streets:
All joy is darkened, the mirth of the land is gone.
And it shall come to pass,
That he who fleeth from the noise of the fear
Shall fall into the pit;
And he that cometh up out of the midst of the pit
Shall be taken in the snare:
For the windows from on high are open,
And the foundations of the earth do shake.
The earth is utterly broken down,
The earth is clean dissolved,
The earth is moved exceedingly.
Then the moon shall be confounded,
The sun shall be ashamed,
And the earth shall reel to and fro like a drunkard,
And shall fall, and shall not rise again.
And all the host of heaven shall be dissolved,
And the heavens shall be rolled together as a scroll:
And all their host shall fall down,
As the leaf falleth off from the vine,
And as a falling fig from the fig tree.
The waters shall fail from the sea,
And the rivers shall be wasted and dried up.

Streams of water shall be turned into pitch,
And the dust thereof into brimstone,
And the land thereof shall become burning pitch.
And the smoke shall not be quenched by night or day,
And no man shall pass through it.
But the cormorant and the bittern
Shall possess the land;
The owl also and the raven shall dwell in it.
And there shall stretch out upon it
The line of confusion, and the stones of emptiness.
They shall call the nobles thereof to the kingdom,
But none shall be there,
And all her princes shall be nothing.
And thorns shall come up in her palaces,
Nettles and brambles in the fortresses thereof:
And it shall be an habitation of dragons,
And a court for owls.
The ambassadors of peace shall weep bitterly,
And the highways shall lie waste.
The glory of the forests shall be consumed,
And the fruitful field;
Yea, the trees shall be so few,
That a child may count them.
Behold, the day shall come,
That all that is in the earth,
And all that which thy fathers have laid up in store,
Shall be carried up in smoke,
For ye have forgotten thy Heavenly Father
And thy Earthly Mother,
And ye have broken the Holy Law.
Oh that thou wouldst rend the heavens,
That thou wouldst come down,

That the mountains might flow down at thy presence.
When thy hand showed forth the power of thy Law,
Thou camest down in fury:
The mountains flowed down at thy presence,
And the melting fires burned.
Behold, thou art wroth, for we have sinned.
We are like the troubled sea, when it cannot rest,
Whose waters cast up mire and dirt.
We trust in vanity, and speak lies;
Our feet run to evil,
Wasting and destruction are in our paths.
We grope for the wall like the blind,
We stumble at noon day as in the night,
We are in desolate places as dead men.
But now, O Heavenly Father, thou art our father:
We are the clay, and thou our potter,
And we are all thy people.
Thy holy cities are a wilderness,
Thy forests are consumed,
All thy earth is a desolation.
Our holy and beautiful house
Where our fathers praised thee,
Is burned up with fire.
Even the ancient lore of our Father Enoch
Is trampled in the dust and ashes.
And I beheld the earth, and, lo,
It was without form, and void;
And the heavens, and they had no light.
I beheld the mountains, and, lo, they trembled,
And all the hills moved lightly.
I beheld, and, lo, there was no man,
And all the birds of the heavens were fled.

I beheld, and, lo, the fruitful place was a wilderness,
And all the cities thereof were broken down
At the presence of the Lord, and by his fierce anger.
For thus hath the Lord said,
The whole land shall be desolate;
Yet will I not make a full end.
Behold, the hand of the Law is not shortened,
That it cannot save;
Neither is the ear of the Law heavy,
That it cannot hear:
From out of the desert shall I bring forth a seed,
And the seed shall be planted
In the Garden of the Brotherhood,
And it shall flourish,
And the Children of Light shall cover the barren land
With tall grass and trees bearing fruit.
And they shall build the old waste places:
They shall repair the waste cities,
The desolations of many generations.
They shall be called the repairers of the breach,
And the restorers of paths to dwell in.
They shall be a crown of glory on the head of the Lord,
And a royal diadem in the hand of the Law.
The wilderness and the solitary place
Shall be glad for them,
And the desert shall rejoice, and blossom as the rose.
It shall blossom abundantly,
And rejoice even with joy and singing.
The eyes of the blind shall be opened,
And the ears of the deaf shall be unstopped.
Then shall the lame man leap as an hart,
And the tongue of the dumb shall sing:

For in the wilderness shall waters break out,
And flowing streams in the desert.
And the parched ground shall become a pool,
And the thirsty land springs of water.
And an highway shall be there, and a way,
And it shall be called the Way of the Law:
The unclean shall not pass over it,
But it shall be for the Children of Light
To cross over the Eternal River unto the hidden place
Where standeth the Tree of Life.
And the children of men shall return to the earth,
And come unto the Infinite Garden
With songs and everlasting joy upon their heads:
They shall obtain joy and gladness,
And sorrow and sighing shall flee away.
And it shall come to pass in the last days,
That the mountain of the Lord's house
Shall be established in the top of the mountains,
And shall be exalted above the hills;
And all the sons of men of the earth shall flow unto it.
And many people shall go and say,
Come ye, and let us go up to the mountain of the Lord,
To the tabernacle of the Holy Law,
And the Holy Angels will teach us
Of the ways of the Heavenly Father
And the Earthly Mother,
And we will walk in the paths of the righteous:
For out of the Garden of the Brotherhood
Shall go forth the Law,
And the word of the Lord from the Children of Light.
And the Lord shall judge among the nations,
And shall rebuke many people:

And they shall beat their swords into plowshares,
And their spears into pruninghooks:
Nation shall not lift up sword against nation,
Neither shall they learn war any more.
Hear the voices of the Brothers,
Which cry aloud in the wilderness:
Prepare ye the way of the Law!
Make straight in the desert a highway for our God!
Every valley shall be exalted,
And every mountain and hill shall be made low:
And the crooked shall be made straight,
And the rough places plain:
And the voice of the Heavenly Father shall be heard:
I, even I, am the Law; and beside me there is no other.
Yea, before the day was I am he:
And there is none that can deliver out of my hand.
Hearken unto me, O Children of Light!
I am he; I am the first, I also am the last.
Mine hand also hath laid the foundation of the earth,
And my right hand hath spanned the heavens.
Hearken unto me, O Children of Light!
Ye that know righteousness,
My children in whose hearts is my Law:
Ye shall go out with joy, and be led forth with peace:
The mountains and the hills
Shall break forth before you into singing,
And all the trees of the field shall clap their hands.
Arise, shine, O Children of Light!
For my Light is come upon thee,
And thou shalt make the Glory of the Law
To rise upon the new earth!

THE ESSENE WAY: *AN INVITATION*

If you found this book meaningful, you may be interested to learn more about THE ESSENE WAY, a renaissance of the ageless values of the first century Essenes, translated into creative and constructive 20th century life styles.

Over the years, thousands upon thousands of truth-seekers from all over the world have written to us, asking for the opportunity to study and put into practice the Essene teachings in a harmonious framework, in the company of those motivated by similar ideas and ideals. In response to this need, *The Essene Way*, in cooperation with Academy Books, Publishers, now conducts an annual Essene Seminar and Workshop, attended every summer by students from all over the United States and abroad.

If you would like to know more about next summer's Essene Seminar and Workshop, or if you are interested in a comprehensive home study program, please write to *The Essene Way,* care of Academy Books, Publishers, 3085 Reynard Way, San Diego, California 92103, for our usual *spring* announcement.

The Essene Seminar also provides training for future teachers and ministers. We cordially invite those who are seriously interested to write to *The Essene Way.*

Peace be with you!

Books by EDMOND BORDEAUX SZEKELY on the Essene Way of Biogenic Living

THE ESSENE WAY—BIOGENIC LIVING. The Essene-Biogenic Encyclopedia.	$8.80
DISCOVERY OF THE ESSENE GOSPEL OF PEACE. The Essenes & the Vatican.	4.80
SEARCH FOR THE AGELESS, I: My Unusual Adventures on Five Continents.	7.80
SEARCH FOR THE AGELESS, II: The Great Experiment.	8.80
SEARCH FOR THE AGELESS, III: The Chemistry of Youth.	7.50
THE GREATNESS IN THE SMALLNESS. Meditations of a Philosopher.	7.50
THE TENDER TOUCH: BIOGENIC SEXUAL FULFILLMENT.	5.50
THE BIOGENIC REVOLUTION. The 1977 International Essene Seminar.	9.50
BIOGENIC REDUCING: THE WONDER WEEK.	3.80
THE ESSENE BOOK OF CREATION. Light on the Mystery of Mysteries.	4.50
TEACHINGS OF THE ESSENES FROM ENOCH TO THE DEAD SEA SCROLLS.	4.80
THE ESSENE JESUS. Revaluation of the Latest Essene Master and his Teachings.	4.50
THE ESSENE BOOK OF ASHA: JOURNEY TO THE COSMIC OCEAN.	7.50
THE ZEND AVESTA OF ZARATHUSTRA. Powerful Universal Masterpiece.	4.80
ARCHEOSOPHY, A NEW SCIENCE. Beginning of the Beginnings.	4.80
THE ESSENE ORIGINS OF CHRISTIANITY. 100 Facts and 200 Fallacies.	7.50
THE ESSENES, BY JOSEPHUS AND HIS CONTEMPORARIES.	1.80
THE ESSENE TEACHINGS OF ZARATHUSTRA. Immortal Legend of the Wheat.	1.80
THE ESSENE SCIENCE OF LIFE. Companion Book to the Essene Gospel of Peace.	3.50
THE ESSENE CODE OF LIFE. The Natural and Cosmic Laws.	2.80
THE ESSENE SCIENCE OF FASTING AND THE ART OF SOBRIETY.	2.80
COSMOTHERAPY OF THE ESSENES. Unity of Man, Nature and the Universe.	2.80
THE LIVING BUDDHA. A Comparative Study of Buddha and Yoga.	4.50
TOWARD THE CONQUEST OF THE INNER COSMOS.	6.80
JOURNEY THROUGH A THOUSAND MEDITATIONS. 8000 Years of Wisdom.	9.50
FATHER, GIVE US ANOTHER CHANCE. Survival Through Creative Simplicity.	6.80
THE ECOLOGICAL HEALTH GARDEN, THE BOOK OF SURVIVAL.	4.50
THE DIALECTICAL METHOD OF THINKING. Key to Solution of All Problems.	2.50
THE EVOLUTION OF HUMAN THOUGHT. 87 Great Philosophers, 38 Schools.	1.95
MAN IN THE COSMIC OCEAN. Where No Man Has Ever Gone.	2.80
THE SOUL OF ANCIENT MEXICO. Hundreds of Ancient Pictographs.	7.50
THE NEW FIRE. Renewal of Life in a Precolumbian Spiritual Rhapsody.	4.80
DEATH OF THE NEW WORLD. Children of Paradise. 200 Illustrations.	4.80
ANCIENT AMERICA: PARADISE LOST. Pictorial Encyclopedia of a Lost World.	4.80
PILGRIM OF THE HIMALAYAS. Discovery of Tibetan Buddhism.	1.95
MESSENGERS FROM ANCIENT CIVILIZATIONS. Ancient Migrations.	2.50
SEXUAL HARMONY. A Lucid, Common-Sense Approach.	3.50
LUDWIG VAN BEETHOVEN, PROMETHEUS OF THE MODERN WORLD.	1.95
BOOKS, OUR ETERNAL COMPANIONS. Culture, Freedom, Tolerance.	2.50
THE FIERY CHARIOTS. The Mysterious Brotherhood of the Dead Sea.	4.80
CREATIVE WORK: KARMA YOGA. Ancient, Mystic Role of Creative Work.	1.95
THE ART OF STUDY: THE SORBONNE METHOD. The Joy of Learning.	2.50
COSMOS, MAN AND SOCIETY. Guide to Meaningful Living in the 20th Century.	5.80
I CAME BACK TOMORROW. 20th Century Nightmare and the Essene Dream.	2.80
BROTHER TREE. Charming Ecological Parable for Children of All Ages.	2.80
CREATIVE EXERCISES FOR HEALTH AND BEAUTY.	2.95
THE BOOK OF LIVING FOODS. A Gastro-Archeological Banquet.	3.50
SCIENTIFIC VEGETARIANISM. Nutritional, Economic, Spiritual Guide.	2.50
THE CONQUEST OF DEATH. Longevity Explored. The Dream of Immortality.	1.95
HEALING WATERS. Fifty European Spa Treatments at Home.	3.50
PREVENTIVE DIET FOR HEART AND OVERWEIGHT. Charts and Recipes.	3.00
TREASURY OF RAW FOODS. Menus, Meals, Recipes.	1.95
THE BOOK OF HERBS. Complete Informative Reference.	2.50
THE BOOK OF VITAMINS. THE BOOK OF MINERALS. Each Volume:	1.95
THREE TALKS: Thought-Provoking Lectures of Edmond Bordeaux Szekely.	2.50

Write for Free Complete Descriptive Catalogue to the International Biogenic Society:
I.B.S. International, Apartado 372, Cartago, Costa Rica, Central America

Book orders must be prepaid. Add 10% for postage & handling (min.order:$3.00, min. postage:50¢). Make check in US currency out to I.B.S. Internacional. Please use Air Mail!